BISBEE

The University of Arizona Press

Tucson & London

BISBEE

Urban Outpost on the Frontier

Edited by Carlos A. Schwantes

With the assistance of Tom Vaughan

The frontispiece is from a 1914 panoramic
view of Bisbee in the heart of the Mule
Mountains. Bisbee Mining and Historical
Museum: Accession No. 85.2.1.

The University of Arizona Press
Copyright © 1992
Arizona Board of Regents
All Rights Reserved
Printed in Japan by Dai Nippon Printing Co.

96 95 94 93 92 5 4 3 2 1

LIBRARY OF CONGRESS
CATALOGING-IN-PUBLICATION DATA
Bisbee : urban outpost on the frontier / edited
    by Carlos A. Schwantes, with the assistance
    of Tom Vaughan.
        p.   cm.
    A companion volume to a permanent
exhibit of the Bisbee Mining and
Historical Museum.
    Includes bibliographical references
and index.
    ISBN 0-8165-1303-1 (alk. paper). —
ISBN 0-8165-1292-2 (pbk. : alk paper)
    1. Bisbee (Ariz.)—History—Exhibitions.
2. Bisbee (Ariz.)—Description—Views—
Exhibitions. 3. Mines and mineral
resources—Arizona—Bisbee—History—
Exhibitions. I. Schwantes, Carlos A.,
1945- . II. Vaughan, Tom, 1947–
III. Bisbee Mining and Historical
Museum.
F819.B6B57 1992   91-41114
979.1'53—dc20   CIP

BRITISH LIBRARY
CATALOGUING-IN-PUBLICATION DATA
A catalogue record for this book is available
from the British Library.
This book is a companion volume to the
permanent photo exhibit entitled "Bisbee:
Urban Outpost on the Frontier" of the Bisbee
Mining and Historical Museum (Project
Director Larry B. Tanner). The book was
funded in part by the National Endowment
for the Humanities.

Dedicated to Mary and Roberta
with many thanks

Contents

Illustrations

Maps

Preface and Acknowledgments

The town of Bisbee, Arizona, is the historian's delight. During even a brief stroll along its twisting and uneven streets so typical of early mining camps one senses ghosts of the past near at hand. They are present in grand old buildings like the Pythian Castle and the Copper Queen Hotel, nestled in the copper-hued hills of the mining landscape visible from almost every vantage point. But Bisbee is certainly no ghost town.

Few bars now line Brewery Gulch, once the boozy heart of the commercial district, but the larger portion of town now known as Old Bisbee is still very much alive and well. Very few shops stand empty or boarded up. Old Bisbee has never been fatally "malled" by the outlying convenience stores and shopping centers that have so often sucked life out of traditional city centers. Perhaps it has been saved by its cramped layout, but part of what makes Bisbee so remarkable today is that it will most likely stay like it is for many years to come.

Though a living, functioning community in tune with the 1990s, Bisbee is also a remarkable museum that preserves the turn-of-the-century look and feel of the West's once extensive copper kingdom. Its past is visible in its huge Lavender Pit and in the headframes and mine dumps to the south and east, and much of this history is preserved in old photographs and government documents.

No recollection of Bisbee's past stirs more diverse opinions than the infamous deportation of suspected labor radicals in 1917. One thing is certain: townsfolk are not likely to reenact the deportation just to please the tourists. Other western mining centers imitate Walt Disney's Frontierland, but that is not Bisbee. The main tourist attractions are the daily tours through the Queen Mine and the brochures that aid visitors in making self-guided strolls through Old Bisbee. Other than that, Bisbee pretty much leaves a person alone to enjoy the town's rich history in a leisurely and personal fashion.

The Bisbee Mining and Historical Museum is part of that unhurried and understated approach to the town's history. In the recent upgrading of its exhibits, the emphasis was on an honest and educational rendering of Bisbee's past, even the controversial parts. Publication of this book is part of that educational effort. Read it for the historical information it contains, enjoy the photographs and maps, and take it along on a trip to compare the Bisbee of today with the mining town of the past.

In putting this book together I was fortunate to have a fine body of photographs to draw upon; and in Tom Vaughan, curator of the Bisbee Mining and Historical Museum, I had a person who not only knew his collection well but also understood the technical side of photography. I appreciate his help as well as that of the other authors of individual essays. I thank Larry Tanner, former director of the Bisbee Mining and Historical Museum, for initiating this project and seeing it through some difficult times. Lauri Lindsay, museum secretary, and Sherry A. VanDerWerf, museum registrar, provided needed encouragement and assistance. Professor A. Yvette Huginnie of the University of Colorado, Boulder, kindly shared with me the results of her ongoing research into race and ethnicity in Arizona mining towns. For other help along the way, I also want to thank Chris Leischow and Peter Steere of the University of Arizona Library Special Collections and Nancy Dafoe and Marge Pon of the University of Idaho.

Without the support of President Elisabeth Zinser of the University of Idaho and History Department Chair W. Kent Hackmann, I doubt that I would have had the opportunity to undertake editing of this project.

Finally, special thanks go to my wife Mary who literally kept the home fires burning in Northern Idaho and juggled the demands of her career and the raising of our two lively boys during my several research trips to Southern Arizona. Tom and I agree that because of their patience during our total immersion in this project, our wives—Mary and Roberta—deserve to have this book dedicated to them.

CARLOS A. SCHWANTES

Project Director's Comments

As is often the case when we first conceive of a project, we don't fully realize its eventual scope and complexity. So it was in 1987 when we at the Bisbee Mining and Historical Museum began exploring the creation of a new permanent exhibit to interpret the early history of Bisbee. Over the next three years our project increased in complexity to include a gallery renovation, a new exhibit, a range of educational materials, a lecture series, a Spanish-language audio tour, and this book.

Bisbee: Urban Outpost on the Frontier was at first conceived of as the usual exhibit catalog, serving as a permanent record of the exhibit. As the organizing concept of the exhibit itself changed, the book took on a new dimension. Originally, the exhibit was intended to interpret Bisbee simply as local history. As research and planning for the project progressed, it became apparent that a broader organizing concept would more accurately reflect Bisbee's history. Despite its frontier isolation, Bisbee had all sorts of complex ties to the larger world. Local development could best be seen as a result of many larger forces interacting on a regional, national, and even international scale.

Although *Bisbee: Urban Outpost on the Frontier* follows the general organization of the exhibit, it has content entirely its own. It includes broader research, which was helpful in developing the new displays but not included in their text and labels. Also distinct from the exhibit are the illustrations chosen specifically to complement the text of the book. The final product stands on its own merits and will surely endure beyond the life of its parent exhibit. I hope it will serve as a model and stimulus to rethink the presentation of local history by museums and historical societies throughout the nation.

A substantial amount of credit for using the "big picture" concept must be given to the program officers of the National Endowment for the Humanities, who gave us the initial nudge to reexamine our local history in a larger context.

The NEH played another very important role by encouraging us to seek out the highest quality consultants to bring to the project knowledge beyond that of our museum staff. The contents of this volume are a direct result of our seeking this outside expertise in a group of people with varying research backgrounds.

Three of the contributors to *Bisbee: Urban Outpost on the Frontier* worked with our own curator and contributor, Tom Vaughan, as part of our planning team. Clark Spence was sought out for his broad range of research in the American West, which not incidentally included various aspects of mining. Carlos Schwantes, selected for his study of labor in the Pacific Northwest, expressed interest in expanding the geographic range of his research. He brought with him valuable experience as a writer and editor with a keen interest in using historic photographs for their intrinsic information. Richard Graeme's background as mining engineer, along with a long-standing interest in the history of Bisbee and its mines, made him a welcome addition to the team.

LARRY B. TANNER, Director
Bisbee Mining and Historical Museum
1987–1991

BISBEE

Introduction

CARLOS A. SCHWANTES

Bisbee and the Copper Kingdom

A series of urban outposts separated by a vast and sparsely populated expanse of arid land characterized the American Southwest well into the twentieth century. The region's peculiar pattern of settlement is clearly visible on the maps that accompany the 1900 federal census: population that had pushed steadily west from the Atlantic seaboard along a more or less solid front seemed to hesitate and fracture once it reached the dry country beyond the 100th meridian to create hundreds of distinct islands on the land.

One such community was Bisbee, isolated in the canyons of the Mule Mountains of southeastern Arizona, about six miles north of the Mexican border. At an elevation of fifty-three hundred feet and surrounded by hills that topped seventy-three hundred feet, Bisbee was an oasis that received more moisture and less summer heat than the surrounding drylands. Although tourists in the early twentieth century often found Bisbee's mountainous location appealing and even picturesque, the sole reason for its existence was mining, and the story of Bisbee is that of its mines. From them came fortunes in lead, zinc, manganese, gold, and silver—more silver and gold than any other place in Arizona—but copper above all else determined the fate of Bisbee.

"That depends on the price of copper" was a refrain commonly heard on its streets. The mines around Bisbee produced almost eight billion pounds of the red metal during the century that ended in 1981. Copper equaled prosperity or adversity: a rise in price in Paris or the opening of a new mine in Chile would impact life in Bisbee. The lingo of mining was the common language of all residents regardless of economic or ethnic differences.

Bisbee was one of several urban outposts that comprised the copper kingdom of the American West. Among its sister camps were Jerome, Globe, Ajo, Clifton, and Morenci, Arizona; Bingham, Utah; Butte, Montana; Ely, Nevada; and Santa Rita, New Mexico. All

Bisbee's business district wound along the narrow floors of two intersecting canyons: Brewery Gulch, seen here shortly after 1900, and Mule Gulch, now called Tombstone Canyon or Main Street.

were one-industry towns, all rode the roller-coaster of economic boom and bust, and all were visual reminders that the mineral industry of the West was scattered among a number of remote and often nearly inaccessible places.

The West contained approximately 90 percent of the nonferrous metal reserves in the United States. By the eve of World War I it produced the bulk of the nation's copper, and most of its gold and silver. Before the West emerged as a center of copper production, the country's most important source of the red metal had been the Keweenaw Peninsula in far northern Michigan where America's first modern copper mining began in the 1840s.

In the 1870s and 1880s huge deposits of copper were discovered in Montana, which became the nation's leading producer by the end of the nineteenth century. Montana took that title from Michigan in 1887 and yielded it to Arizona in 1910. Arizona remained in first place as leading producer of copper during most of the twentieth century, although Utah, Nevada, and New Mexico also emerged as important producers. Unlike Montana, where copper deposits were concentrated in the Butte area, Arizona's ore bodies were scattered throughout the territory. Bisbee rose to prominence at the site of one major deposit, and by 1900, together with Clifton, Globe, and Jerome, it dominated production in the territory.

For America's copper industry the decade of the 1880s was a time of significant change. That ten-year interval not only saw the emergence of the West as a major copper producer but also the meteoric rise of the electric industry to provide a vital new market. When the decade opened, manufacturers prized copper primarily for its indestructibility. It was a key ingredient in the alloys brass and bronze, and various forms of it appeared in clockworks, cookware, roofing, and protective sheathing on ship hulls. Soon to be recognized was copper's importance as a conductor of electricity.

Like California's placer gold deposits in the late 1840s, the discovery of copper could generate considerable excitement, although the red metal was far less often a poor man's road to wealth than gold might be. If a prospector located a claim, he could sell out and make some money, even a fortune. But the work of actually mining a copper deposit was not for those faint of heart or short of capital. It presented the sort of challenge that could be met only with money and lots of it.

Unlike Michigan's high-grade ore, which scarcely needed smelting to make the copper valuable, western deposits were of a nature that required enormous sums of money before the metal could be mined, smelted, refined, and marketed. Such unprecedented amounts of capital would be difficult, if not impossible, to raise in

The Bisbee of 1890 was an island on the land, hemmed in by the Mule Mountains which rose abruptly from the surrounding plain.

Above Bisbee's business district, numerous residences clung precariously to the hillsides in this 1905 view. Steep roads, trails, and stairways connected the various parts of town. One visitor in 1913 noted: "Its situation is more that of an Alpine village of the old world than a thriving and prosperous city of the new."

Copper was the lifeblood of Bisbee, as this interior photograph of the Copper Queen smelter in the early 1890s illustrates. Although Montana copper production first surpassed that of Michigan in 1887, the dominance of the western state was not firmly established until 1892. Likewise, Arizona first pulled ahead of Montana in 1907 but did not establish an uncontested claim as America's leading copper producer until 1910.

Copper wires crisscrossed a New York City street in the 1880s. When Thomas Edison's first power station began commercial operation near here in 1882 it heralded the dawn of the age of electricity. Countless additional miles of telephone and telegraph wires further stimulated copper production. Whereas telegraph wire had once been made of iron, the industry now turned to copper.

the economically undeveloped and lightly populated West. Thus the copper kingdom—like the frontier West in general—became a colony dependent on an infusion of money from more developed areas.

Investment capital flowed into the region and the products of its forests, fields, and mines flowed out to distant markets. The East supplied money, and the West provided labor and raw materials. Given that the West contained a mere 5 percent of the nation's population in 1900, that relationship was perhaps inevitable, though it denied Westerners any real control over their economic destiny. Because of the huge sums of capital required to develop copper deposits, a few giants dominated the industry, notably, Anaconda in Montana, Kennecott in Utah, and Phelps Dodge in Arizona. By

1940 these three eastern-based companies accounted for 80 percent of the West's copper output.

Without the lure of metal mining it is difficult to imagine anyone challenging the native peoples for possession of the southeastern corner of Arizona. Here was a frontier with little surface water and no direct rail service until the 1880s. Added to these problems was the presence of the warlike Apaches who frightened away would-be settlers or forced new arrivals to take extraordinary precautions for fear of attack. Prospectors dared to scout the area only by working closely with military troops, and occasionally prospectors and soldiers were one in the same. In fact, the first mineral discoveries in the Bisbee area date from 1877, when members of an Army search party from nearby Fort Bowie staked a claim.

These first discoveries quickly evolved into big business. In August 1880 the Copper Queen Mine was capitalized for $2.5 million, and the owners renamed the camp of Mule Gulch in honor of their San Francisco attorney and business associate, DeWitt Bisbee, who according to legend never visited his namesake. At this time the settlement had nearly four hundred inhabitants—many of them young, single males—and could boast of a post office, two saloons, a brewery, three boarding houses, and a general store.

If Bisbee was synonymous with copper it was also inseparable from the names Phelps Dodge and James Douglas. To speak of one was to infer the others. Douglas was the link between the long-established New York and New England mercantile firm of Phelps, Dodge & Company and the raw frontier outpost of Bisbee. Phelps Dodge approached Douglas in 1881 for advice about whether to build a smelter to treat western ores on New York's Long Island Sound. The forty-three-year-old university-trained metallurgist (and self-educated mining engineer), who had only recently returned from an inspection trip to Arizona, advised that future smelters were better located near the mines themselves.

Impressed by its initial contact with Douglas, Phelps, Dodge & Company hired him to serve as their representative in far-off Arizona. It was on Douglas's advice that Phelps, Dodge & Company acquired the Atlanta claim in Bisbee in 1881 and then merged it with the adjacent Copper Queen mine four years later to avoid protracted lawsuits over copper-bearing formations that extended through both claims. When the two properties united in August 1885 they began large-scale operations under the name of the Copper Queen Consolidated Mining Company, for many years the crown jewel in the Phelps Dodge collection of mining properties.

During the next two decades Douglas succeeded in making the Copper Queen a producer of copper second only to the massive

Dr. James Douglas (1837–1918) influenced Bisbee's copper industry more than any other single individual.

Anaconda operation in Butte. In the process he became a multi-millionaire and dominant figure in the rapidly developing copper industry of Arizona and northern Mexico. He also played a role in launching a Phelps Dodge railway empire in the Southwest and in establishing the Arizona city that still bears his family name.

By any measure, Douglas was a remarkable person. A native of Quebec and broadly educated in Canada in several fields, he was a "renaissance man" who made good. Though he was universally known as "Dr. Douglas," unlike his father, a Scottish-born surgeon, he did not have a medical degree. In 1899, however, McGill University in Montreal awarded Douglas an honorary doctorate of laws.

Both of Douglas' sons followed their father into mining, and each left his own mark on the mineral industry of the Southwest. The elder son, James S. Douglas, supervised several mine and railway construction projects, while younger son, Walter, served for a time as general manager of the Copper Queen mine and later became president of Phelps, Dodge & Company.

Two more names were intimately associated with the Copper Queen operation in early Bisbee: the Williams brothers. Lewis "Don Luis" had charge of the smelter, a post he held for fifteen years, and Ben became general manager of the Copper Queen. Both were London-born emigrants who acquired their knowledge of copper mining during an extended stay in the Michigan mines. To make the circle of friends and family complete, it might be added that one of Ben's brothers-in-law was DeWitt Bisbee, and Lewis's daughter married James S. Douglas.

Bisbee remained a Phelps Dodge town until about 1899 when the Calumet & Arizona Mining Company was formed to begin large-scale operation at its Irish Mag mine located adjacent to Phelps Dodge property. Bisbee's third major mining company dated from 1904 and the development of a claim that eventually led to formation of the Shattuck-Arizona Copper Company. Phelps Dodge, however, clearly remained dominant in Bisbee and subsequently acquired its key rivals, notably the Calumet & Arizona Mining Company in 1931.

Bisbee was never a company town in the strictest sense, yet whatever Phelps Dodge did inevitably affected community life. Most houses were privately owned, and in time Bisbee established a municipal government, police and fire departments, and a chamber of commerce, all of which were more or less independent of the company. Yet when townspeople spoke of "the company" they meant Phelps Dodge (or "PD" as it was known locally).

Near the intersection of Brewery Gulch and Tombstone Canyon stood the general offices of PD's Copper Queen Consolidated Mining Company, an imposing red brick structure that now houses the Bisbee Mining and Historical Museum. Across the street "the company" operated a store (originally the Copper Queen Mercantile dating from 1886), which was one of Bisbee's major businesses, although many privately owned enterprises competed directly with it. Phelps Dodge provided the town with its first hospital, school, library, finest hotel, and controlled one of its daily newspapers.

The nature of copper mining not only demanded huge amounts of investment capital but also railroad connections to transport the ore from mines to processing plants and markets. Unlike gold and silver, which were so valuable that they were priced by the ounce and could be easily and profitably transported by pack train or stagecoach to the nearest railhead, copper's much lower value for a given weight required that substantially greater amounts of the red metal reach the market in order to make a mining operation pay.

In its quest for cheap transportation, Phelps Dodge commenced writing its signature in steel rails across the Southwest, tentatively at first and then with bold and impressive strokes. Bisbee's first railroad connection to the outside world was completed in 1889. As the Arizona and South Eastern Rail Road, its tracks wound clockwise around the southern tip of the Mule Mountains to reach a Santa Fe affiliate at Fairbank. The railroad's immediate impact on Bisbee was to reduce the cost of hauling freight; it also influenced daily life by making widely available consumer goods that were once considered unattainable luxuries.

The Southern Pacific declined to build a branch line to the smelter at Douglas, and after a dispute with the Santa Fe over freight rates, Phelps, Dodge & Company continued to extend its railway lines. As the El Paso & Southwestern, the PD's rail empire ultimately evolved into a thousand-mile-long system that crossed the Chihuahuan and Sonoran deserts to link Bisbee with transcontinental connections in El Paso and Tucson and even to coal deposits in northern New Mexico.

Bisbee, like almost all western mining towns, grew through a predictable series of stages. Initially it amounted to little more than a collection of crude dwellings, populated mainly by the single males who worked in the mines and smelters. It was much like its sister camps which were fashioned from tents and crude wooden shacks strung along rough streets hacked into the hillsides. They looked like the temporary communities most of them proved to be. But copper camps, unlike typical gold and silver settlements, sometimes evolved into substantial population centers. As buildings of brick and stone replaced those of wood, places like Bisbee and Butte took on the appearance of modern industrial centers.

Completion of the railroad made it possible for Bisbee's Can-Can Chop House to advertise "Fresh oysters and seafood from the East and California."

Even as Bisbee's physical appearance changed, so did the surrounding hillsides as smelter operations expanded in the 1880s. Crude attempts to smelt ores began as early as 1879 but became large-scale operations after a new smelter was completed in the early 1880s. Trees that once dotted the hillsides were cut down to provide the four thousand cords of wood needed each year for industrial steam and domestic uses before completion of a railroad provided access to new sources of fuel. What woodcutters didn't take, the sulfurous smelter fumes did. By the end of the 1890s the hillsides were nearly barren. The result was a series of disastrous floods, caused in part by the lack of vegetation to check rain water as it cascaded down the slopes.

In the 1890s Bisbee could accurately be described as a filthy, smelly, and smoke-filled camp. Yet even if sulfur fumes filled the air of the enclosed valley, they were not universally regarded as evil. Some people believed that sulfur smoke was beneficial in protecting the community from the ravages of typhoid fever; and even if that assertion was suspect, few could argue that smelter stacks belching smoke were signs of prosperity.

Shortly after the turn of the century, the Copper Queen moved its smelter operation twenty miles east to the new town of Douglas, where copper interests laid out a settlement just north of the Mexican border. In Douglas, ores from Bisbee and Nacozari, Mexico, could be smelted where there was both open space and an ample supply of water. The new smelter commenced operation in 1904, and the old Bisbee facility was closed down and scrapped a few months later.

Bisbee's coming of age as a community dates from the turn of the century when it emerged as one of the West's most lively boom towns. Hundreds of businesses lined its twin canyons, and its streets were full of new faces. When Bisbee was incorporated on January 9, 1902, its population stood at about eight thousand. During the years from 1899 to 1918 the population increased from four thousand to an all-time high of approximately twenty-five thousand.

The flood of 1895 as it raced by the Bisbee landmark of Castle Rock. Bisbee was laid out at the junction of two major watercourses in the Mule Mountains, and though their beds are normally dry, the monsoon rains of July and August can quickly turn them into raging rivers. As recently as July 1986 five automobiles were swept to destruction by waters raging down Brewery Gulch.

The year 1900 forms a convenient dividing line between Bisbee as mining camp and Bisbee as urban-industrial center, aspiring metropolis of the Southwest, and one of Arizona's three largest cities. The Bisbee that emerged from the nineteenth century was by any measure still a dirty, somewhat ramshackle place that more nearly resembled its mining camp past than its urban-industrial future, but that soon changed as the violence, crudity, filth, and drunkenness that typified its past began to disappear after 1900. Each problem yielded to techniques of control as the new century progressed.

It is not surprising that mining camp Bisbee suffered the calamities of repeated floods, fires, and epidemics. Garbage was thrown out the back doors of restaurants, the carcasses of dogs and burros occasionally littered even the main streets, and open cesspools contributed to the problem of pervasive stench, flies, and mosquitoes.

The flood of July 30, 1890, was one of the worst: twenty minutes of rain sent water rushing through the canyons, sweeping two men to

This was the scene in turn-of-the-century Bisbee shortly before smelter operations shifted to Douglas. After the relocation, some locals noted that nothing was left in Bisbee except the pure air of the Arizona desert.

their deaths, and smashing fifteen cabins. Both Tombstone Canyon and Brewery Gulch were watercourses of the Mule Mountains, and when early arrivals stripped the hillsides of their juniper, oak, and manzanita for mining and domestic needs they made the problem of flash floods that much worse. When an underground concrete conduit called "the subway" was completed along the length of Tombstone Canyon in 1909, it helped alleviate the problem of flooding but did not stop it entirely. The same was true of the check dams federal workers built up the canyons in 1936.

A fourteen-mile-long sewer system was completed in 1908 at the cost of $84,000. Another system of pipes brought pure, cold water from Naco six miles away to replace the ubiquitous little burros that once delivered water door to door in canvas bags. Together the clean water and sewage disposal facilities helped Bisbee win the battle with disease. During these turn-of-the-century years of modernization, the wooden Bisbee of the 1880s and 1890s was reconstructed of more substantial building materials such as brick, block, and stone. Replacing commercial buildings with less combustible materials reduced the threat of fire, but did not eliminate it completely.

As Bisbee evolved physically, it changed socially. It became a city of families as more and more newcomers arrived with wives and children. Bisbee stores now advertised the latest in fashions for both men and women. The coming of families, in turn, intensified efforts to clean up the physical environment, control disease, and eliminate the vices that seemed most closely associated with the city's saloons. At one time Bisbee had about fifty saloons, some fifteen of which were located in Brewery Gulch, long the haunt of a floating population of tramp miners, gamblers, con artists, and prostitutes who congregated in its saloons. In time both its saloons and its vices were tamed. In fact, the first municipal ordinance passed after the incorporation of Bisbee banned all women from saloons. Subsequent city and state laws prohibited gambling (1907), prostitution (1910), and liquor (1915).

After the incorporation of the Bisbee Improvement Company in 1900, Phelps Dodge, along with other mine owners, bankers, and railroad men had a hand in establishing or improving electrical, natural gas, and telephone service to the town's residents. Telephone and electric lines soon extended to all parts of the growing city. Another important symbol of the modern age, the automobile, first appeared on Bisbee streets in 1900.

Bisbee formed a Chamber of Commerce in October 1905 to sell itself to a world that knew little about the community except for its mines. Boosters could now point with pride to the splendid new Muheim Building which soon boasted of a stock exchange with

In the early twentieth century, Mexican entrepreneurs delivered water door to door by burros at the cost of fifty cents a bag (approximately eighteen gallons to a bag).

the latest market reports from New York City. They were proud, too, of the Copper Queen Hotel, a luxurious seventy-five-room Mediterranean-style structure.

Only a few months after the luxury hotel opened for business on February 22, 1902, it hosted an important gentleman from Indiana, Senator Albert J. Beveridge, chairman of the Committee on Territories. He and several other members of his committee spent three days in Arizona during a whirlwind inspection tour of the Southwest. He reached Bisbee on November 20.

Despite a friendly reception, Beveridge returned to Washington still firmly opposed to statehood for Arizona, an area he regarded as backward and dominated by mining companies. The Indiana Senator would, however, support the admission of Arizona and New Mexico as a single state, an arrangement Arizonans overwhelmingly opposed. Despite this blow to their hopes, Arizonans continued to make statehood a chief topic of public discussion.

When the Copper Queen Hotel opened its doors in 1902, it offered first-class accommodations worthy of a metropolis many times the size of Bisbee.

The great fire of 1908 was the largest and most costly conflagration in Bisbee history. It left five hundred people homeless and destroyed more than half the commercial buildings along Main Street.

At the center of this panoramic view of Bisbee is the Copper Queen Hotel. Directly in front of it is the general office building of the Copper Queen Consolidated Mining Company, now the Bisbee Mining and Historical Museum. These two structures are landmarks that can still be used to orient visitors to Bisbee. At the right of the Copper Queen is the entrance to Brewery Gulch, and Bisbee's Main Street business district extends out of the photograph to the left.

On the same day, September 6, 1905, at which time it was the largest city in Arizona, Bisbee played host simultaneously to territorial conventions of the Republican and Democratic parties. Naturally, the main issue was statehood, a goal Arizona finally attained on February 14, 1912.

Even as Arizona achieved greater political integration into the federal union, Bisbee's physical ties to distant states and cities proceeded apace as a result of a growing network of railroad, telephone, and telegraph lines. In mid-1916, the high-point of the railroad era, the El Paso & Southwestern teamed up with the Southern Pacific and the Rock Island lines to run luxury trains from Chicago and St. Louis to Los Angeles and San Francisco by way of southeastern Arizona. Five trains a day each way linked Bisbee with the main line at Osborn (seven miles southeast of town) where a person could board the Golden State Limited.

The desert was still forbidding, but passengers could cross it in comfort in sleeping cars and the "Library-Buffet-Observation Car" that brought up the rear of the Golden State Limited. More ad-

venturesome souls could drive their automobiles to Los Angeles along the "Borderland Route," a transcontinental highway completed through Bisbee on the eve of World War I. Considering the rigors of the trip, few people at the time could have predicted that private automobiles would eventually eliminate passenger train service to Bisbee and most other western communities.

Giving everyday life in Bisbee a cosmopolitan quality were Serbian, Irish, Welsh, Cornish ("Cousin Jacks"), Italian, Hispanic, and other immigrant groups. Various national and religious festivals and holy days reflected a rich ethnic heritage. Conspicuously missing, however, were Chinese, barred from settlement by unwritten law based on popular hostility. Bisbee, as a consequence, was often called a "white man's camp."

The community was likewise unabashed in its class distinctions, from Quality Hill, location of some of Bisbee's most substantial homes, to Tintown, an across-the-tracks Hispanic settlement. South Bisbee was a workers' enclave that was home to numerous Welsh and Italian miners. Other suburbs included Don Luis, Lowell, and Bakerville.

As Old Bisbee grew, satellite communities developed that together with Bisbee comprised the Warren Mining District. The most impressive of these was Warren itself, a planned community that the Calumet & Arizona Company began constructing on the plain just southwest of old Bisbee in 1907. Each home was connected to modern electric, water, and sewer systems. The most elegant residence belonged to Walter Douglas, whose Italianate mansion was strategically placed to command a sweeping view of Warren and the surrounding plain. The new suburb could boast of a children's park and baseball field. Water pumped from the mines made Warren a green oasis in stark contrast to the surrounding desert.

When a streetcar line was completed from downtown Bisbee to Warren in March 1908, it was the occasion for a major display of community pride. Thousands of residents turned out for a grand celebration. A mile-long extension was later built to take riders farther south to the country club. Located just north of the Mexican border, it featured tennis courts, a rifle range, shooting traps, and a nine-hole golf course.

Even with its country club, no one could ever forget Bisbee's principal reason for existing: within sight of the fine new homes were the headframes of mines, supply areas, freight wagons, and trains. Some twenty-five headframes dotted the landscape in 1910, and nearby were multihued piles of waste rock and a maze of tracks, trestles, and embankments over which steam locomotives puffed busily twenty-four hours a day.

This map of the Warren Mining District ca. 1912 shows the location of Old Bisbee relative to the planned community of Warren.

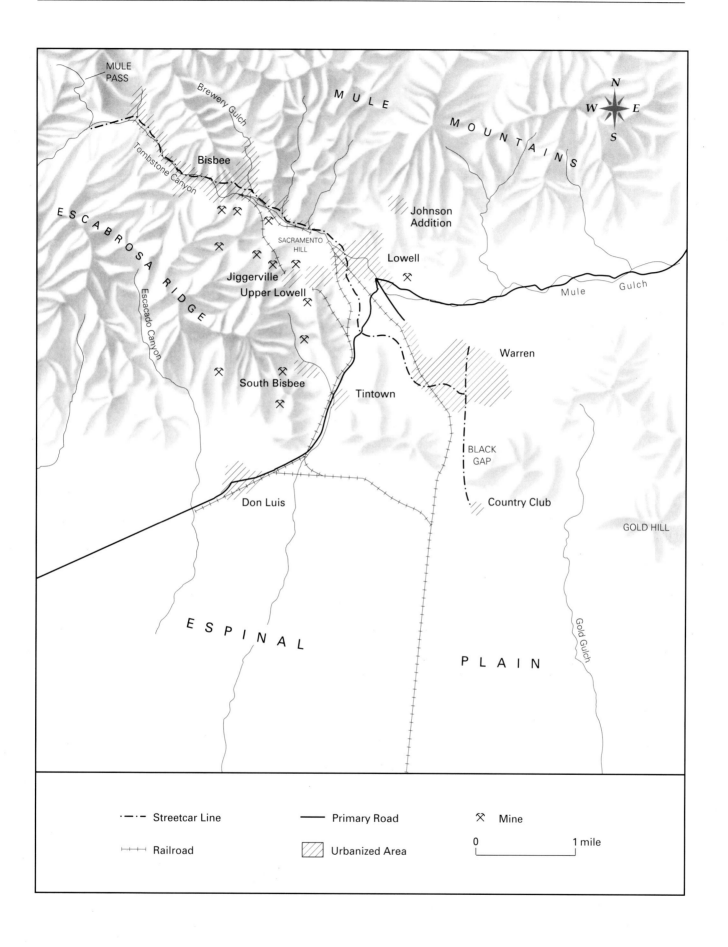

MULE PASS

Brewery Gulch

MULE

MOUNTAINS

N
W   E
S

Tombstone Canyon

Bisbee

Johnson
Addition

SACRAMENTO
HILL

Lowell

ESCABROSA

Mule   Gulch

RIDGE

Jiggerville

Upper Lowell

Escacado Canyon

Warren

South Bisbee

Tintown

BLACK
GAP

Country Club

GOLD HILL

Don Luis

Gold Gulch

E S P I N A L

P L A I N

-·-·- Streetcar Line   —— Primary Road   ⚒ Mine

+—+—+ Railroad   ▨ Urbanized Area   0   1 mile

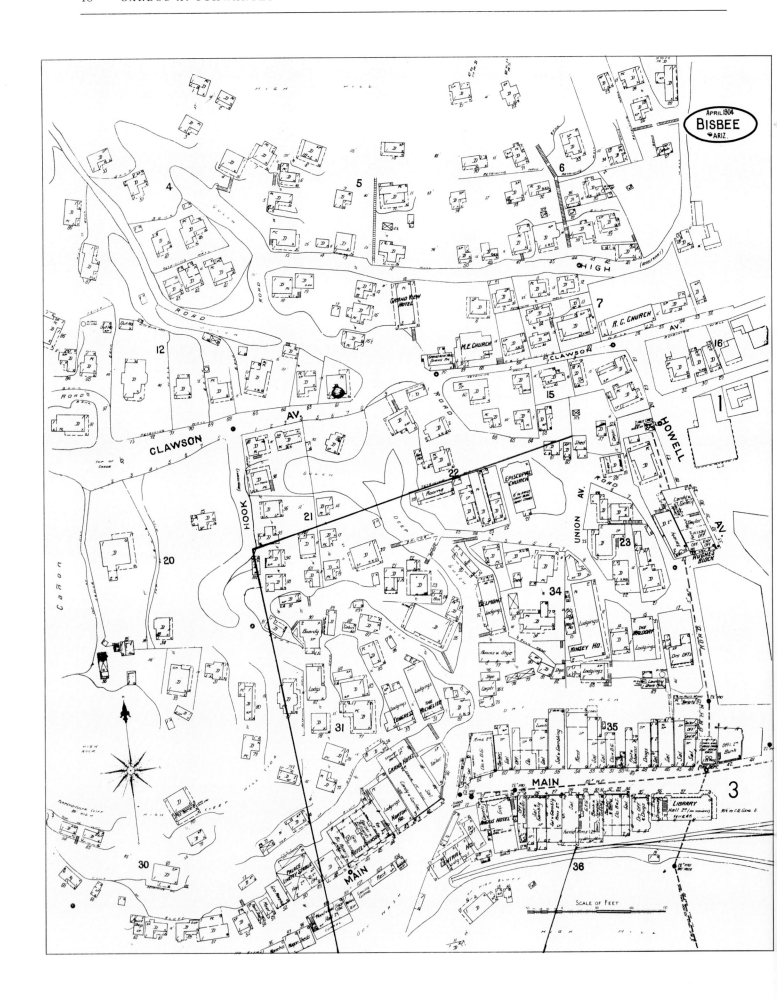

Street maps of Bisbee and Warren illustrate dramatic differences between the physical layouts of the two towns: the irregular pattern of Bisbee contrasts with the more regular pattern of Warren. The average price for a lot in Warren originally was approximately three hundred dollars. Courtesy: Bisbee Mining and Historical Museum

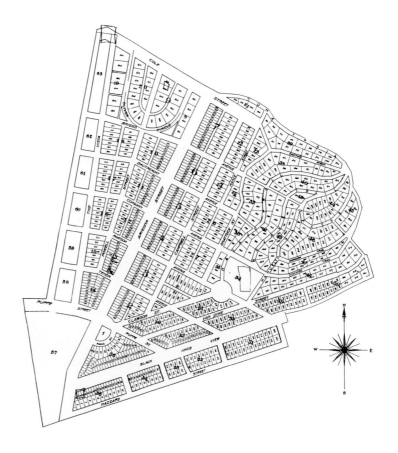

In 1913 the population of Bisbee and its suburbs was approximately nineteen thousand. At that time the mines of the Copper Queen, Calumet & Arizona, and Shattuck-Arizona companies employed six thousand men and shipped more than thirty-five thousand tons of ore a week to smelters in Douglas. The monthly payroll in the district in 1913 was reported at $750,000 of which the big three mining companies paid $500,000.

With the eight-hour workday in effect since 1902 and the mines paying good wages, workers had both the time and money necessary to enjoy a variety of activities during their off-duty hours. Although membership in the country club was beyond the reach of most workers, there were still the lodge and fraternal meetings, banquets, dances, concerts, plays, picnics, baseball games, and patriotic celebrations like the Fourth of July. Another day worth celebrating was the tenth of each month, payday for many miners throughout Arizona.

When the world war came to Bisbee in April 1917, it gave rise to yet another visible dividing line in the community's history. Highlighting the war years were increasing copper prices, a rising cost of living, and a bitter labor dispute that Bisbee would never forget. Probably nothing did more to shatter community cohesiveness

Brass bands were a popular way to cele-brate special occasions. Seen here is the Calumet & Arizona band. Employees of the Copper Queen also had a band.

Bisbee residents took a holiday to celebrate completion of their new streetcar line in 1908. Not only could they ride in comfort instead of walking a long distance in the summer sun, but the new streetcar line symbolized modernity and prosperity for their community.

than the infamous deportation of nearly twelve hundred alleged labor radicals in July 1917. This event effectively marked the end of Bisbee's exuberant years of growth, excitement, and innocence. By the time the war ended, hatred of organized labor had spread throughout Arizona, a state once noted for its friendliness to trade unions.

Symbolizing the dramatic changes the war years brought to Bisbee was the explosion that occurred only days after the deportation and blasted the top off Sacramento Hill. It signaled the start of a new era of open-pit mining. The old Bisbee landmark vanished, and a huge crater emerged in its place as Bucyrus steam shovels chewed relentlessly through the earth. Daniel Jackling had pioneered the open-pit method at his Bingham, Utah, operation in 1907 as a way to recover low-grade, finely disseminated copper deposits and still make a profit. Open-pit mining not only left an unmistakable mark on Bisbee's landscape but also on its work force by substituting machines for much of the human labor formerly required in underground mines.

Before Phelps Dodge halted work in 1929, some thirty-four million tons of rock and earth had been removed from the Sacramento Pit. Until it acquired the adjacent properties of Calumet & Arizona in 1931 the company was unable to expand its operations.

Phelps Dodge started digging a second and even larger pit in 1950, just south of the old Sacramento Pit, and named it for its general manager, Harrison Lavender. Production commenced in 1954, and the concentric rings of the Lavender Pit spiraled slowly

Long after it disappeared from the mines, the hand-drilling tradition was maintained by contests that often formed the centerpiece of Fourth of July celebrations in early twentieth-century Bisbee. Blocks of granite imported from Gunnison, Colorado, insured uniform hardness for all contestants, some of whom were professionals from out of town.

DRILLING AT BISBEE 4TH JULY

outward to encompass most of the suburb of Lowell as well as the Sacramento Pit. The Lavender Pit closed in late 1974.

The following year, for the first time in almost a century, the demands of mining did not determine the pace of life in Bisbee. The closing of all underground mines and the Lavender Pit created depressed conditions. A number of businesses, including the Phelps Dodge Mercantile, the "company store" in downtown Bisbee, shut their doors for good. Phelps Dodge relocated many of its employees to corporate operations in Ajo, Morenci, and Safford, Arizona, and Tyrone and Playas, New Mexico.

In the resulting slump, miners' homes could be purchased for as little as $1,000. By 1981 retirees constituted 41 percent of Bisbee's eight thousand residents, with a small but visible counterculture—called "hippies" by some—accounting for part of the rest. More and

By June 1918 Bucyrus steam shovels had already removed one shoulder of Sacramento Hill. Bisbee is seen in the distance.

more, Bisbee's economy came to depend on the arts and the small but growing business of selling history by which the town sought to attract tourists to see its colorful and still very visible past.

Bisbee's heritage is recorded in its mining landscape, historic buildings, legal documents, folk reminiscences, and photographs. Some of the thousands of photographs preserved by the Bisbee Mining and Historical Museum are displayed on these pages.

From 1880 to 1920 more than thirty professional photographers recorded the affairs of the evolving mining community. One of them was L. A. Nemeck, whose studio is seen here at the turn of the century. A large skylight helped provide illumination for taking indoor portraits with the slow film of the era. The octagonal structure, which was not actually attached to Nemeck's studio, served as a practice room for Bisbee bands.

Copper Star of the Arizona Urban Firmament

CHARLES S. SARGENT

Arizona is preeminently an urban state. It always has been, and the state's history is essentially that of the many towns and cities that are the focus of Arizona's social, economic, and political development. With the notable exception of the presidios of Tubac (1752) and Tucson (1776), both founded while Arizona was part of the Spanish colonial empire, the state's urban system developed only after the American Civil War.

Many of the post-1865 towns were mining camps. Some of these, particularly copper camps like Bisbee that had an abundance of rich ores, grew into permanent towns and cities. Scores of other settlements became "ghost towns." A ghost town was typically a small gold and silver boom town that had exhausted its shallow economic base.

Still other Arizona towns began as agricultural centers, with mining districts forming their major initial markets. A few towns arose along the roads that connected fields and mines, and beginning in the 1880s a number of settlements sprouted alongside transcontinental railroads as they extended their lines across Arizona. Branch track eventually linked the principal mining centers and farm towns to main lines.

While mining, agriculture, commerce, and transportation were the dynamos that powered Arizona's early economic and town growth, the need for frontier law and official records made some of these settlements important county seats as well. There was, however, little manufacturing in Arizona's young towns, and the bulk of activities such as brewing, baking, ice-making, and metal-working met mainly local needs. Most manufactured goods arrived from distant cities, which, thanks to America's expanding railroad network, also formed an enormous national market that permitted the development of large-scale copper mining, profitable cattle ranching, and diversified agriculture in the Southwest.

Josiah Muirhead, an immigrant from Canada, was Bisbee's first mayor. He and his wife pose in C. S. Fly's studio.

Arizona's towns and cities, like those of other western states, were outposts on the frontier of the American West. Nonetheless, it is unlikely that any place in North America, even in the colonial years, was ever sufficiently isolated to have originated in a closed, local system. Throughout its history the fortunes of Bisbee were linked to influences beyond its boundaries.

The Gold Rush to California after 1848 saw an increasing number of Euro-Americans from distant locations traveling across southern Arizona. They ferried the Colorado River at Camp Yuma, established in 1848, and by 1854 a settlement had been laid out on the Arizona shore. But it was only after the Civil War that a town actually developed there and only in 1873 that it took the name Yuma. Goods shipped by sea around Baja California from San Francisco and destined for Tucson and Arizona's army camps and mining centers arrived at the new port by river steamboat. Small volumes of rich copper ore from the Southwest were shipped from Yuma to England via San Francisco for a short time after 1854.

It was gold and silver, however, that initiated creation of a complex Arizona townscape and made Yuma the most important of many river landings. After 1863 a number of mining towns evolved in the Bradshaw Mountains of central Arizona, and small steamboat landings along the Colorado River grew to serve them. One of these, Aubrey's Landing, had a small smelter and served a short-lived copper operation at Planet.

The Searchlight, *a Colorado River steamboat, docks at the foot of Main Street in Yuma in the early twentieth century. Part of the territorial prison is visible on the bluff in the distance.*

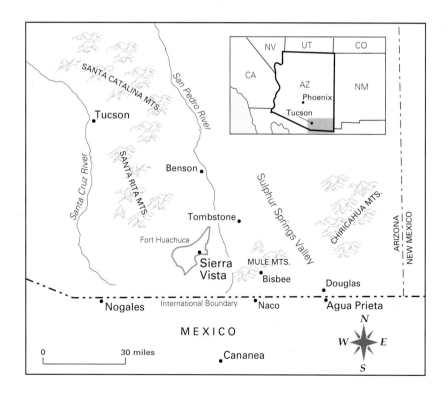

Key urban areas in southeastern Arizona in the 1990s.

Characteristic of a mining frontier and the lubricity of fortune, the earliest camps were impermanent in nature and eclectic in architecture. The typical assortment of dwellings ranged from tents and lean-to's to adobe and wood-framed structures. Few such settlements survived to become part of Arizona's modern urban system. One that did was Wickenburg, born of the 1863 discovery of the rich Vulture gold deposit. Soon becoming one of the largest settlements in Arizona, it vied with Tucson for territorial capital upon separation of Arizona from New Mexico Territory in 1863.

That political plum fell to Prescott the following year, purposefully created in the center of the territory, on the edge of the active Bradshaw mining districts, and adjacent to newly sited Fort Whipple. By 1873 there were seventy-three hundred gold or silver mines and a handful of towns in the area. One of these, Bradshaw City (1871), was briefly the second largest town in Arizona before it faded away. Like the nearby mining towns, Prescott was linked by the Colorado River port of La Paz to San Francisco, Arizona's major trading partner.

At the time of his first surrender in 1886, the famous Apache leader Geronimo requested that his photograph be taken by Tombstone (and later Bisbee) photographer C. S. Fly. Geronimo is mounted on the left; also on horseback is Naiche, son of Cochise. Geronimo escaped shortly after this only to be recaptured two months later and exiled to Florida.

The end of the Civil War saw the rapid reappearance of the military in Arizona. For the next quarter century the United States Army was actively involved in Indian affairs, with its major assignment being to carry out federal policy whereby native Arizonans were to be systematically "pacified," "removed," and "concentrated" on newly delineated reservations. Although federal "removal" policies initiated early in the 1870s were popular with Euro-Americans throughout Arizona, Indians reacted with violence. In southeastern Arizona, soldiers from Fort Bowie (1862–94) and Fort Huachuca (1877–   ) played an active role in restraining the Chiricahua Apaches. Their leader, Geronimo, finally surrendered not far from Bisbee in 1886. Thereafter, the farmers, ranchers, and miners who spread out across Arizona had only to worry about marauding bands of Mexican bandidos and American cattle rustlers. A local response was the establishment of the Arizona Rangers in 1901.

For nearly three decades the small military camps and larger forts provided important markets for Arizona merchants and farmers. Until the Indian wars ended in the mid-1880s, federal military expenditures, along with silver and gold mining, were the major elements of the Arizona economy.

Military materiels, mining equipment, tools, clothing, and even some basic food items arrived at Arizona's small forts and towns from San Francisco and also in increasing amounts from major cities of the Atlantic seaboard. Meeting the need for hay and foodstuffs (victuals or "vittles")—particularly flour, fresh vegetables,

Patrolling the nation's military frontier in the mid-1880s were the soldiers stationed at Fort Huachuca. Of Arizona's several dozen Army camps and forts of the 1880s, only Fort Huachuca, located twenty-five miles west of Bisbee, remains active today.

and meat—was another matter, given the cost and difficulty of transporting bulky or perishable items a long distance to Arizona. A growing population of cattle, horses, and humans spurred development of the territory's own agricultural potential and the rise of farm towns. Following the example of irrigated agriculture long practiced by peaceful Indians along the Gila River, Florence grew after 1866 as an exemplary "vittleville" tied to the Tucson market.

The Florence example was, in turn, duplicated farther north along a road linking Tucson with the mining districts of Wickenburg and the Bradshaw Mountains. Here the combination of Wickenburg capital, the water of the Salt River, the example of abandoned Indian canals, the success of Florence, a proximate market at Camp McDowell, and the growing markets of the mining districts proved irresistible. Two years after the first crops were planted in 1868, the vittleville of Phoenix was laid out. Nearby Tempe, begun by a Tucson merchant, followed in 1871, and the inexorable march of Utah Mormons across northeastern Arizona led to the founding of Mesa in 1878, the third Euro-American settlement in the Salt River Valley. From Mesa a handful of Mormon dissidents headed farther south to the San Pedro River Valley and settled St. David.

In some mining districts, rich copper deposits soon superseded gold and silver. The 1872 camps of Clifton and Morenci quickly focused on copper, and in 1873 the small settlement of Solomonville arose to supply mesquite charcoal for the small Clifton copper smelter. Globe and nearby McMillanville grew as silver centers on land excised in 1876–77 from the 1871 San Carlos Indian Reservation, but by 1880 Globe's future was tied to copper. The Clifton-Morenci mining district had even earlier been withdrawn from the Indian reservation. Along the upper Gila River, Safford (1874) and Thatcher (1883) evolved as Mormon farming centers with the copper towns to the north forming important markets.

The railroad also played an important role in shaping Arizona's urban firmament. America's Civil War delayed completion of the nation's first transcontinental railroad until 1869, and the two trunk lines across Arizona were built only in the early 1880s. Southern Pacific tracks crossed southern Arizona, while those of the Santa

Fe traversed northern portions of the territory. The northern route led to the founding of Holbrook, Winslow, Flagstaff, Williams, and Kingman in 1882 and 1883. A branch line south from Ash Fork aided development of the copper industry at Jerome.

Large-scale copper production would have been equally impossible at Bisbee and Globe or Clifton and Morenci without the Southern Pacific line, which in Cochise County alone gave rise to Benson, Willcox, Bowie, and San Simon in 1880 and 1881. Other branch lines reached the copper towns of Clifton in 1884 and Globe in 1898. All of these new lines brought in consumer goods and equipment for the copper operations (including coke for the smelters) and hauled Arizona copper to eastern markets.

Railroads equally served the agricultural towns that victualled both the mining districts and more distant markets. West of Casa Grande (1879), another new Southern Pacific station—Maricopa—was the stop for stages to Phoenix before the 1887 opening of the Maricopa and Phoenix Railroad (via Tempe) provided the basis for new agricultural centers, including Glendale (1892) and Scottsdale (1896). A county seat since 1871, Phoenix gained the territorial capital from Prescott in 1889, and by 1900 Maricopa County—the Salt River Valley and Wickenburg—had the largest population in Arizona.

It was within the context of this urban frontier that a Fort Bowie party searching for Apaches discovered silver in the Mule Mountains in 1877 and filed the district's first mining claim at the Pima County seat of Tucson. The handful of prospectors who entered Mule Gulch the following year increasingly focused their attention on the area's rich copper deposits. Their young mining camp became Bisbee in 1880.

Early Bisbee was overshadowed, however, by the 1877 discovery of rich silver deposits that gave birth to Tombstone, located about twenty-five miles northwest of the copper camp. Within a year the population of Tombstone had climbed to almost one thousand (compared to Bisbee's four hundred); the boomtown became the seat of newly established Cochise County in 1881. (Only in 1929, after Tombstone's long decline, would county government shift to Bisbee.)

The Bisbee of 1880, like other Arizona settlements at the time, was on the verge of becoming more closely tied to the modern urban-industrial world. It gained direct rail access to the outside world when a thirty-six-mile line to Fairbank, the nearest railhead, opened in 1889. During the 1880s Bisbee grew from a tentative camp of a few hundred residents to a town of two thousand, the center of large-scale exploitation of copper in Arizona and a grow-

Fort Bowie, established during the Civil War in 1862, became a base of Army operations against the Apaches. A search party led by Lieutenant Anthony Rucker located mineral outcroppings at a site in the Mule Mountains that became Bisbee. The army outpost was abandoned in 1894.

Tombstone as it appeared during the heyday of its silver mines in the 1880s. The old Cochise County courthouse appears at the upper left of the photograph. For many tourists today, Tombstone with its numerous false-front buildings and wooden sidewalks epitomizes the mining frontier.

ing trade center for ranches in the area. By the turn of the century it would have approximately six thousand residents.

At that time Bisbee vied with Tucson to become the most populous settlement in Arizona, but because basic urban amenities were slow to reach the copper camp, it could scarcely match either Tucson or Phoenix in appearance, comfort, or economic diversity in 1900. Electric service did not extend to most Bisbee residences and there were no private telephones. The town also lacked a bank; instead, various mercantile establishments provided basic financial services.

Bisbee in 1900 was commonly described as a smelly, dirty, and smoke-ridden camp. At that time it still had no pavements, sewers, or municipal water system. Its drinking water was polluted by the proximity of wells to privies and stables. Even wastes from some of the "better homes" flushed directly into roads and gullies, and in some places human excrement spread out across yards and sloshed down hillsides. Slops and garbage were thrown randomly about. Housewives also had to deal with dust, flies, sulfur fumes from the smelter, and the smoke of green firewood.

The Herculean task of cleaning this Augean stable was most commonly carried out (perhaps providentially) by fire and flood. Major fires in 1885, 1886, and 1887 were inspired by the widespread use of wood construction, but after the railroad arrived in 1889 the growing use of imported brick for commercial structures tended to lessen both the frequency and impact of fire.

The floods remained inevitable, however, not only because the stores and dwellings of the 1880s clustered along the bottom of Tombstone Canyon and Brewery Gulch—the two distinct central zones of the town—but also because the natural environment had been rapidly and fundamentally altered. In the absence of coal, the juniper, oak, and manzanita that covered the slopes above town quickly became fuel for heating, household cooking, and industrial steam. Also helping to keep the hillsides barren were the process of locating mining claims and the sulfurous fumes from the smelter. Consequently, nothing checked heavy rainfalls.

Particularly between 1900 and World War 1 Bisbee acquired its character as a modern Arizona city. In 1900 the formation of the Bisbee Improvement Company (closely linked to Phelps Dodge) slowly led to extension of electric service throughout the town (the mines had long before been electrified). The Bisbee Improvement Company also took responsibility for providing gas, telephones, and ice. Long distance telephone service reached the Mexican mines at Cananea by 1901. Telephone links to a wider Arizona came after 1910 when a holding company of Bell Telephone bought the local exchange.

Cowboys herd Mexican longhorns across the international border into Cochise County near Palominas ca. 1910. The animals were probably destined for the railhead at Hereford, a few miles northeast.

Local goals of modernity, improved public health, and the promotion of trade took form after Bisbee's 1902 incorporation as a city. Building codes and fire protection were soon in place and by 1904, the year of the first municipal elections, potable water from nearby Naco, Sonora, in Mexico, was available to the public. In 1908 a fourteen-mile municipal sewer system was in place, and by 1909 the major streets were paved. Underground was the new "subway," a large and miles-long concrete conduit designed to channel the floodwaters that periodically disrupted Main Street.

From the 1890s Main Street was the town's primary shopping street, and it was here that most new commercial buildings were erected after 1900. Located on the non-copper side of the "Dividend Fault" that runs down the floor of the canyon (and later through Lavender Pit), downtown Bisbee was spared having to blend commercial structures with mine headframes or pits. The Bank of Bisbee (1900), Bisbee's first, and the Bank of Douglas (1902) became influential "copper bankers" who joined with outside financiers to shape Arizona. In time, they became part of Valley National Bank, today the largest in-state bank in Arizona.

Brewery Gulch, the secondary downtown focus, had always been "different" from Main Street. The 1881 brewery itself was torn down in 1904, but about one-third of Bisbee's fifty bars were here, as were perhaps one hundred "soiled doves" who worked in the Gulch's licensed bawdy houses. When prostitution was declared illegal in 1910, it resurfaced at Naco, a 1901 railroad town located just across the Mexican border. When prohibition came to Arizona in 1915, it also favored business in Naco.

As Bisbee became a "family town," an increasing number of churches took root on the residential hillsides. To a certain extent, the different churches reflected the complex social geography of Bisbee. As a mining town, there had always been racial discrimination, and Bisbee was still more of an ethnic stew than a melting pot of Cornish, Welsh, Italian, Slavic, Mexican, and other immigrants. Different hillsides and valleys were the focus of distinct ethnic groups. Income, of course, also fractionized neighborhoods.

A reporter from Tucson said of Brewery Gulch in 1905, seen here a year later, "The street is somewhat frightful from a sanitary point of view. It is covered with slime several inches deep and about four feet wide, from which comes a nauseating odor. Someday Bisbee may have a sewage system and Brewery Gulch will be clean and wholesome and will not smell to heaven."

By the early twentieth century, Bisbee was popularly described as "three miles long, three blocks wide and three acres high."

As new mines opened, even more residential districts appeared. Among them were South Bisbee (strongly Italian and Welsh), the Johnson Addition, Jiggerville, and the Mexican barrio of Tintown. Lowell quickly developed as a thriving commercial district two miles from downtown Bisbee. Elsewhere, the small neighborhood of Tovreaville grew up next to a meat packing plant. Don Luis evolved at a rail junction.

The planned "company town" of Warren was laid out six miles south and a thousand feet lower than Bisbee. The fan-shaped addition was developed by a subsidiary of the Calumet & Arizona Mining Company. The town's lots—first sold in 1906—were hooked up to both water and sewer. There were also wide streets, sidewalks, street lights, and spacious yards, none of which were yet

Bisbee residents search for bodies after the flood of July 1890. The water-filled barrels seen atop several dwellings were designed to provide fire protection. If a building caught fire, according to local legend, a person was supposed to shoot holes in a barrel to start the water flowing.

Canned food lines the walls of Gus Hickey's store in Brewery Gulch ca. 1910. The number and variety of items brought to Bisbee for local consumption symbolize how the railroad connections that linked the town to the national market could change local shopping and eating habits.

common in Old Bisbee. A range of architectural styles—principally Neo-classical, Bungalow, Mission Revival, and Craftsman—appeared over the next two decades, with the large and elaborate houses of mining executives being erected along the Vista, a linear park. Phelps Dodge purchased the Warren Company in 1917.

The separate towns were in reality functional subdistricts of Bisbee, particularly after the 1908 opening of the Warren-Bisbee Street Railway that linked the two termini (via the intervening small towns) with a thirty-minute, ten-cent ride. Bus service replaced the trolley line in 1928.

The combined Bisbee district (the Warren Mining District) had a population of fifteen thousand by 1910; ten years later that figure would reach an all-time high of approximately twenty-five thousand. In 1959 all of the outlying centers would be legally incorporated into the modern city of Bisbee, which has a population today of slightly less than sixty-five hundred, according to the 1990 census.

By 1920 the Arizona economic base was easily recited by school-children as the five "c's"—copper, cattle, citrus, climate, and cotton. The largest "c" stood for copper. By 1910 Arizona had permanently surpassed Montana as the nation's leading copper producer. Many of the state's politicians were said to wear "copper collars," passing legislation at the bidding of the copper companies and "copper bankers" that increasingly dominated the state.

The economic and political influence of copper was clearly mirrored by Arizona's townscape, and until the 1930s about half of the state's ten largest cities were copper centers. Some of them were new towns as well. One was Douglas, a planned city sited in 1901 as a smelting center for both Bisbee and Mexican copper and named to honor the Phelps Dodge mogul. Smelters were "blown in" in 1902 by Calumet & Arizona and 1904 by the Copper Queen.

South of Globe, new copper finds and Arizona political pressure persuaded Congress in 1902 to excise even more copper lands from the 1871 San Carlos Indian Reservation. One result was the rise of Winkelman (1905), Christmas, and Hayden (1909). Not far to the northwest, Superior (1902), Ray (1909), and smaller Sonora sprang up, and in 1910 the "Concentrator City" of Miami was platted seven miles from Globe. Near Jerome a new smelter gave rise by 1914 to the company town of Clarkdale, named for Montana copper king and sometimes United States Senator, William Andrews Clark. In 1917 a second smelter created nearby Clemenceau, today part of the farm village of Cottonwood. Elsewhere, short-lived copper towns arose at Sasco, Swansea, and Bagdad. By 1914, Bisbee and other copper towns were well positioned for the rising copper prices that came with World War I.

The modern town of Ajo was born in 1917 when the Calumet & Arizona Mining Company began production at its new open-pit mine. The open-pit method was among the newest technological innovations to alter Arizona's copper landscape. These included advances in explosives, earth-moving equipment, and chemistry that allowed the exploitation of low-grade (less than 2 percent copper) ores. Bisbee began excavation of the Sacramento Pit in 1917, and Jerome's pit opened the following year. The open-pit approach was inevitable and irreversible because World War I effectively stripped the older underground mines of their richest and most easily exploited ores. The new technologies led to large concentrators and ever-larger smelters that increasingly located the total copper labor force in fewer towns.

Although copper significantly shaped the Arizona urban landscape, other new towns also appeared. Gold created Goldfield and Oatman in the mountains west of Kingman in the years 1903 and

Tintown was an impoverished neighborhood that derived its name from the extensive use of metal in the buildings. It housed many of Bisbee's Mexicans and Mexican Americans.

1904, and later finds raised Oatman to a population of more than eight thousand at the peak of the boom in 1924. In southern Arizona, the silver boom town of Arivaca briefly blossomed. Agricultural expansion, particularly in the Salt River Valley, led to numerous new farm towns, including Gilbert (1910) and Chandler (1912). Litchfield Park (1916) developed as a Goodyear company town to coordinate growing the long-staple cotton necessary for wartime tires and airplane fabric. By 1920, Phoenix surpassed both its archrival Tucson and Bisbee in population.

Today, about half the population of Arizona lives in metropolitan Phoenix, which comprises the many towns of the Salt River Valley. Another 25 percent live in metropolitan Tucson and the bulk of the remainder in smaller cities and towns. Bisbee is today one of those smaller outposts.

The evolving place of Bisbee in the hierarchy of Arizona's cities is a reflection of changing times and economies. Particularly since World War II, mining employment in Arizona, as nationwide, has been declining relative to jobs in the growing service and high-tech industries. The mining industry employed more than 7 percent of Arizona's labor force in 1939, but less than 1 percent by 1986. Bisbee's last major copper operation, the Lavender Pit, closed in 1974, and all the town's mines were shut down by the following year. In

anticipation of copper's decline, the town had been losing population since the mid-1960s. The number of jobs in Arizona agriculture also plummeted, from 33 percent of the state's employed in 1939 to just 3 percent by 1986. Few real cowboys now shop or drink in Bisbee; today they are replaced by an occasional soldier from nearby Fort Huachuca.

The economic foundation that Bisbee needed to survive the change was provided ultimately by "hippies" and the retired, by tourism and local pride, by government jobs in Bisbee and work for "outcommuters" in Sierra Vista and Douglas. Starting in the mid-1970s, the "counter-culture" brought with it the arts and crafts that initially alienated locals weaned on mining. Retired residents imported pension and Social Security checks. Tourists increasingly filled shops, restaurants, and rooms. With these changes also came increased concern with environmental degradation. The clean air that followed the 1987 closing of the smelter in Douglas that was either unwilling or unable to meet EPA air standards did not go unnoticed. Today, the "threat" of renewed copper mining in Bisbee is a matter of some concern; not a few would prefer instead to see an industry based on expanded medical services in a community that could attract even more retirees.

By 1980 some 41 percent of Bisbee's population was retired. In part this reflected the number of resident ex-miners, but it also mirrored the overall growth of Arizona's elderly population. As late as 1940 there were but 24,000 people in Arizona over age 65; by 1960 the total had risen to 100,000, and by 1980 some 300,000. By 1980 their share of Arizona population (11.3%) for the first time matched the national average. And while the creation of Sun City (1960) and Green Valley (1962) or even modest Sunsites (1961) north of Bisbee caught the attention of the press, Bisbee was quietly gaining popularity with the in-migrant retiree.

Growing pride in Bisbee's architectural heritage has been matched by awareness of the visual and economic benefits of historic preservation. Today, the old liabilities of Bisbee's slow growth since 1930 have been transformed into new assets. The preserved "quaintness" of the residential districts and the fine pre-World War I buildings that were neither significantly disfigured or replaced by growth are a key to Bisbee's economic future. Bisbee created its first tourist brochure in 1900, established a chamber of commerce in 1905, and since the 1920s, when highway, rail, and air access opened Bisbee to the nation, has sought to draw the tourist with the "Bisbee—It's Different" campaign.

Downtown Bisbee today has perhaps the finest architectural integrity of any city in Arizona. In stark contrast are the downtowns of Phoenix and, particularly, Tucson, which have fallen victim to the "success" of uncontrolled and undirected growth. Flagstaff and Jerome both live by tourism, and, like Bisbee, show concern for preservation and conservation of their historic buildings.

Bisbee has been considerably more fortunate than most Arizona mining centers. Early Morenci and Ray not only declined but were razed to make room for open-pit operations. Clifton, Superior, Miami, and Globe struggle to develop a viable economic base apart from copper while Kearny, Hayden, and San Manuel are still tied to the vagaries of copper prices and corporate paternalism that were once the hallmarks of Bisbee.

What goes around comes around. Bisbee's survival today depends on outside influences, just as it did in the copper era. But unlike most other copper cities, Bisbee is now positioned, both economically and philosophically, to adapt to the changes demanded of modern Arizona.

The Queen and Her Court

RICHARD W. GRAEME

An Industrial History of the Warren Mining District

It was the quest for gold and silver, not copper, that caused army scout and prospector Jack Dunn to pause and look more closely at the rust-stained hills he found in Arizona's Mule Mountains. Precious metals, not base ones like copper and lead, made men rich. Gold and silver had long been avenues to wealth for the fortunate few who found them. Their intrinsic value together with the fact that their finder could at least start developing a gold or silver claim with very little capital made them a prospecting target much preferred over copper.

One advantage of gold and silver over copper was particularly obvious in areas remote from railroad connections, places like the Mule Mountains in the 1870s. Consider the fact that a mule could easily carry to market a month's production from a small gold or silver mine. Such was definitely not the case for the base metals: it took as much as 150 pounds of smelted copper to equal the worth of one ounce of gold or fifteen ounces of silver. Thus, practicality dictated that until cheap transportation opened up a region, only the most valuable metals could be exploited. The Western mining industry thus had its beginning in precious metals; the region's copper deposits, by contrast, seemed to have but modest promise.

That equation changed during the 1880s. The tracks of the Southern Pacific Railroad began their eastward reach across Arizona Territory in 1878 and within two years had forged a vital new transportation link to the West Coast. Also in 1880 the Atchison, Topeka, and Santa Fe Railroad entered the territory from the east. For remote Arizona settlements they brought the promise of a new era of prosperity.

At almost the same time, rapid industrial development in the eastern United States created a seemingly insatiable market for raw materials such as iron, copper, and lead. The number of new industrial and consumer applications for these metals surged, particularly

Two miners pose beside a three-ton specimen of malachite and azurite taken from the Copper Queen Mine. It was displayed at the Chicago World's Fair of 1893.

for copper, which saw new uses in brass for shell cartridges, quality hardware, and most significantly as an excellent conductor of electricity. In the 1880s the use of copper in electrical lighting as well as in the transmission of power and speech (telephone) boomed.

There can be no doubt that had copper remained relatively expensive, the development of these new applications would have been significantly impeded. Copper entered the 1880s at a price of 25 cents a pound and exited at 14 cents a pound, a 40 percent decrease in price despite unprecedented demand. Domestic consumption of copper during the decade increased from 91 million pounds to 231 million pounds annually. It was largely the mines of the West that accounted for the increased availability of the red metal and its significantly reduced price. In 1882 it cost Michigan mining companies an average of 16.8 cents to produce a pound of copper, while the Copper Queen of Bisbee could produce the same amount for 9 cents. By 1889 the Michigan cost averaged 11 cents a pound while that of the Copper Queen was just under 8 cents.

The copper deposits that Jack Dunn and other seekers of gold and silver inadvertently located in the Mule Mountains were rich even by Western standards. For the first year of operation the ores averaged 23 percent copper and 13.5 percent copper for the next four years. Also, the early Bisbee ore was easy to smelt and free from troublesome elements such as arsenic and antimony.

Even with these exceptional features, the true value of the district was not clear in the beginning. Geologically, the origin and extent of Bisbee's rich copper deposits remained uncertain until the early years of the twentieth century. At first, prevailing wisdom was that because so much of Bisbee's ore was found in limestone formations, the copper deposits were of little value. James Douglas reminisced of his first visit to the Copper Queen in 1881: "I could not have thought well of it at that time, because we professional men thought that [ore in] limestone was invariably a fake and was simply placed there by Providence in order to delude us."[1]

Because of this geological peculiarity and the immense amount of capital that would be required to develop the Copper Queen property, the original owners had but one desire and that was to sell. They found their buyer in Edward Reilly who paid them twenty thousand dollars, a small fortune in 1880. The original discoverers of what would become one of the world's greatest mines would share little in its success, but they had risked comparatively little.

Reilly had no money of his own to make the purchase. His plan was to interest others in the property enough to have them advance him the necessary capital yet still allow Reilly to retain a significant interest. At this time there was no capital of consequence in Arizona and for that matter, little was to be had anywhere between

This underground view of the Copper Queen Mine was taken by C. S. Fly in 1883. It shows a small portion of what would become miles of square-set timbers used to protect against cave-ins. The opening to this mine is still visible on the hillside above Old Bisbee.

Lieutenant Anthony Rucker along with his scout Jack Dunn and packer Ted Burns jointly filed the first mining claim in the Mule Mountains in August 1877, marking the beginning of Anglo involvement in the mining district.

Chicago and the West Coast. San Francisco investors, however, had provided much of the money needed to develop the Comstock lode in Nevada, as well as several other western mines. Reilly borrowed enough money to travel to San Francisco in an attempt to float his mine in the remote Mule Mountains. He must have been a competent salesman because he succeeded in selling the Copper Queen to two railway contractors, William Martin and John Ballard, through the mining firm of Bisbee, Williams and Co., while retaining one-half interest as his reward.

Mining in Bisbee now began in earnest with Martin personally overseeing early development work. A smelter was built under the supervision of Lewis Williams, who used a furnace of his own design. Operation of the mine and smelter complex was an unqualified success.

Early involvement of Eastern capital in Bisbee increased significantly when, upon the recommendation of James Douglas, Phelps, Dodge & Company, a New York-based, old-line mercantile firm purchased the Atlanta claim adjacent to the Copper Queen. The Atlanta had no ore on the surface, as did the "Queen," but Douglas could not believe that only one such ore body existed or that an arbitrarily drawn claim line would cut the Atlanta off from the rich ores found on the Copper Queen next door.

The price of the Atlanta claim was forty thousand dollars, a princely sum for untested ground. Douglas's recommendation to buy the property was not without reservation. He advised D. Willis James and William E. Dodge, Jr., "that the risks were too great to be taken by a purchaser who was not able and prepared to lose all that he had invested."[2] Phelps, Dodge & Company accepted the risk and entered the mining game. The decision would change a successful mercantile company into one of the world's largest mining firms.

As if to test the company's resolve, early work on the Atlanta was anything but successful and seemed likely to confirm Douglas's worst fears. For two long and vexing years Douglas searched for ore without luck. James and Dodge had spent eighty thousand dollars on exploration to this point and had nothing to show for it, a fact not very encouraging to Eastern investors in Bisbee mines.

Douglas's faith was badly shaken: not only had he been completely unsuccessful in his quest, but the magnificent Copper Queen ore body ended abruptly before it reached the Atlanta claim. Yet even after these years of arduous work and failure he was still able to persuade the reluctant James and Dodge to commit another fifteen thousand dollars for one final effort, a 400 foot deep shaft. Fate intervened: the shaft struck the top of a rich ore body at 210 feet and continued through the ore for another 200 feet. Almost simultaneously the Copper Queen cut into a continuation of the same ores on their property with a passageway (or drift) from the 400 level.

Now, however, there was the potential for a dispute of the "law of the apex." That law, simply put, permitted the owner of the apex (or top) of a vein, lode, or formation to continue to mine along it even if the ore body extended under claims held by others. To avoid the protracted and expensive litigation over the apex of the ores that so frequently cursed other western mining districts under similar circumstances, the two groups merged into the Copper Queen Consolidated Mining Company.

One year later, in 1886, Phelps, Dodge & Company purchased those shares of the Copper Queen Consolidated Mining Company held by Martin and Reilly. Now the entire output of this fabulous

This view of Bisbee shows the Copper Queen smelter in full operation. Sacramento Hill, later leveled by open-pit mining, looms through the smoke.

mine was controlled by Eastern capital. But control was not enough. As the price of copper continued to decline, new ways had to be found to lower costs. One obvious step was to increase production. A larger smelter was built, as was a plant to concentrate low-grade carbonate ores. Both steps were taken in the face of the lowest price for copper ever seen. Were it not for faith in the Copper Queen and the financial strength of its Eastern backers, Bisbee's mines may well have closed, as many did throughout the West at the time. The stubborn commitment demonstrated by Phelps, Dodge & Company was rewarded many times over as metal prices recovered and the capital invested in new and more efficient technology lowered production costs.

Even so, additional steps had to be taken to keep the Copper Queen profitable. The cost of bringing in supplies such as the heavy mine timbers, immense amounts of which were needed to support the miles of underground passageways, and coke needed by the smelter had to be trimmed as did the cost of shipping semi-refined (black) copper to Eastern markets. A railroad link was needed to connect Arizona's major copper producer with the outside world. Yet when Dr. Douglas approached the Santa Fe, requesting that they build a line into Bisbee, he was treated with "supreme indiffer-

ence."[3] This was despite the fact that every day the railroad handled a hundred tons of freight for the Copper Queen.

The Copper Queen had but one choice—to build a railroad itself, and this it did. Less than two years after the Santa Fe spurned Douglas, a new Bisbee rail link was completed from a connection with the Santa Fe at Fairbank. The cost was in excess of $475,000, most of which was financed by Eastern capital. The impact of this new carrier, the Arizona and South Eastern, was immediate. Freight costs dropped from the $6 per ton by wagon to $1 per ton by rail. Additionally, new sources of supply for the many items required for mine and smelter operation were tapped, further lowering material costs.

Mine timbers now arrived more cheaply from distant Oregon than from the nearby Chiricahua Mountains. A higher quality coke was brought from Trinidad, Colorado, to replace the inferior, but closer San Pedro, New Mexico, product. Equipment and other materials were easily brought from the foundries and mills of both the East and West coasts. Thanks to their new railroad connections, the Bisbee mines not only fed the American industrial machine but became significant consumers of its finished products as well.

The Copper Queen became justifiably famous as Arizona's largest and most profitable copper mine. Rich mineral bodies continued to be found, and with the flow of high-grade ore seemingly endless, the company's position in the district was unchallenged, its future secure. These facts combined with the magnificently spectacular ore specimens available for inspection by would-be investors in distant places, attracted world-wide attention to the Bisbee area. Mining promoters, speculators, and genuine mine operators soon began to look at the Mule Mountains as a place to ply their trade, honest or otherwise.

Properties located miles from the Copper Queen with absolutely no promise or indication of copper were bought by investors as pure stock plays. Quickly separating the unwary capitalist from his money, unscrupulous promoters flagged their properties as the next Copper Queen, which, after all, was but a few miles away and was almost certainly connected by veins of high-grade copper. Many barren holes scattered throughout the Mule Mountains remain mute testimony to these dishonest men and their gullible backers.

Still other men came to develop mines. Most prominent among these was the group of investors that ultimately formed the Calumet & Arizona Mining Company. They gained a foothold through the purchase of the Irish Mag claim, named for a Brewery Gulch prostitute. Through peculiar circumstances this fifteen-acre block of ground had been shunned by Dr. Douglas. He refused to deal with

Weary workmen pose in one of Bisbee's mines in 1910 to illustrate the drilling technique known as double-jacking.

its insane owner, who had threatened the life of his superintendent, Ben Williams. Moreover, there was no hint that there might be any ore on the Irish Mag claim. Further encumbering the "Mag" was a protracted legal dispute that arose when its owner fled town after killing a deputy sheriff.

By 1899 when title to the Irish Mag was settled and its potential for good ore was more apparent, the Lake Superior and Western Development Company (a Calumet & Arizona–related firm backed largely by Pittsburgh-area steel and iron barons) bought the claim from Martin Costello for $500,000. After several anxious and expensive years of development, a fabulous ore body was found on the 1,050-foot level of the Irish Mag. This sent the Calumet & Arizona on a mine property buying spree, acquiring all the promising land it could. Dr. Douglas, not to be outdone by his upstart rival, followed suit and paid a fortune for property considered worthless just a few years before.

All of Calumet & Arizona's efforts could have been for naught and their valuable mine lost had not James Douglas and the partners of Phelps, Dodge & Company initiated an effort to avoid poten-

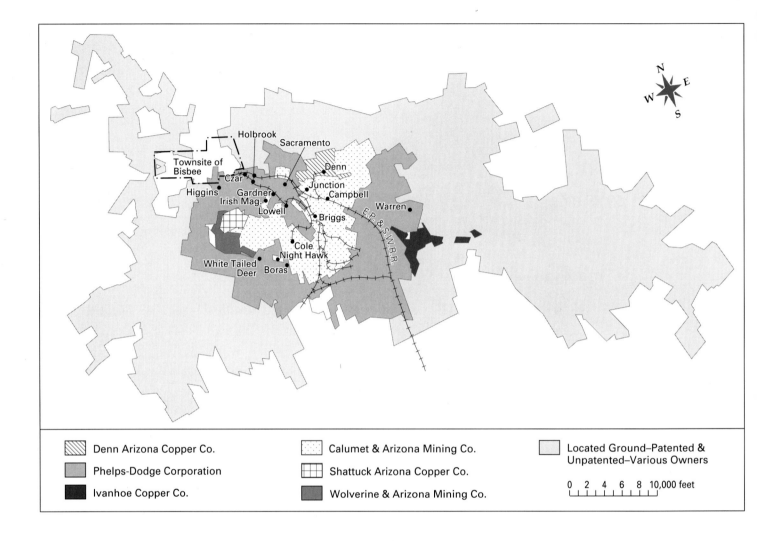

Denn Arizona Copper Co.

Phelps-Dodge Corporation

Ivanhoe Copper Co.

Calumet & Arizona Mining Co.

Shattuck Arizona Copper Co.

Wolverine & Arizona Mining Co.

Located Ground–Patented & Unpatented–Various Owners

0 2 4 6 8 10,000 feet

tially thorny disputes involving "the law of the apex." Problems with this controversial law had been averted once before by consolidating potential rivals. Now, however, that was impossible because Calumet & Arizona was too large for Phelps Dodge to buy out. The Copper Queen believed it clearly held title to the apex of Bisbee ores, but lawyers and courts had a way of clouding titles in western mining camps.

Any conflict between the Copper Queen and Calumet & Arizona would have resulted in lengthy and enormously expensive legal battles, much to the delight of the ever present, predatory lawyers. But before that happened the two companies reached an agreement whereby claim boundaries were projected vertically so as to serve as property lines and each party was granted free access to the other's mines. Thus, Bisbee was once again spared the grief and hatred that so scarred many of the great mining areas of the West.

Soon another player of consequence entered Bisbee's mining game. He was Lemuel Shattuck, a long-time Bisbee resident and saloon keeper who owned a small group of claims a mile south of

Warren Mining District in 1921, showing the complicated nature of claim boundaries. The Atlanta and Copper Queen properties are listed under Phelps Dodge holdings. Courtesy: Bisbee Mining and Historical Museum

the original Copper Queen and beyond any known ore body. With the success of the Calumet & Arizona on previously unproductive ground, Shattuck was able to interest a group of capitalists from St. Paul, Minnesota, in developing his claims. In March 1904 the Shattuck-Arizona Copper Company was formed and by August of that year had located a good ore body. The Shattuck mine was to become an unqualified success paying out more than $8 million in dividends by 1921.

Shattuck, along with Maurice Denn and others, also had a block of claims very much to the east of any known ore bodies. Inspired by success at the Shattuck mine, the Denn-Arizona Copper Company was formed in 1905 with many of the same investors. This time the prize was not so easily won. The ores were deep, with the first located at a depth of seventeen hundred feet. Most of all there was water in amounts never before found in the Warren Mining District. Several times during its development, this mine, called the Denn, was flooded and closed until new, larger pumps could be installed. It was years before the mine made a profit. Later, in 1925, the two companies merged to form the Shattuck-Denn Mining Company. By this time, ironically, the Shattuck mine was largely depleted, but the Denn now turned a handsome profit.

The Copper Queen's chief rival was the upstart Calumet & Arizona, whose mine operations are shown here in 1906.

All across the United States during the early years of the twentieth century there was an increased emphasis on mechanization of
mines, mills, and factories. This was in part a response to a pro-
nounced shortage of skilled labor as American industry expanded
rapidly. If the mining industry could replace skilled labor with machines, it expected to increase productivity and employ men with
lower skill levels.

The first and undoubtedly the most important advance in the
mechanization of mine labor was the pneumatic rock drill. Likewise, electric trolley locomotives were brought underground to move
six or more loaded ore cars at a time to centralized hoisting shafts.
The new technology replaced dozens of the carmen who formerly
pushed a single loaded car to the closest shaft for hoisting. In 1905
there were thirteen shafts hoisting ore by cars in the Warren Mining District. By 1915 there were but five shafts, though they moved
even more ore to the surface.

A new Copper Queen smelter was "blown in" at the southern end
of the Sulphur Springs Valley in 1904 to process ores from Bisbee.
The works had a capacity of 10 million pounds per month, three
times that of the old plant in Bisbee. A townsite laid out in 1901 to

*Mule skinners hauled ore to the surface.
When this picture was taken around 1910,
the ground beneath Bisbee was a honey-
comb of passageways. A hundred or so mules
were kept stabled underground. The first
electric locomotives were used in Bisbee in
1908 and by 1930 had completely replaced
the mules.*

Phelps Dodge employed steam shovels and standard-gauge railroad track for ore and waste haulage from the Sacramento Pit. The date is November 30, 1917, five months after open-pit mining began at this site.

support the new facility was appropriately named Douglas in honor of the man who had so ably led the Copper Queen for twenty years.

Development of the Sacramento Pit began in 1917 by what was then technically the Copper Queen Branch of Phelps Dodge Corporation. This was one of the earliest open-pit mines in the United States. The Sacramento Pit produced nearly 8 million tons of ore yielding in excess of 300 million pounds of copper from 1923 to 1929. Also, nearly 24 million tons of waste rock were removed to access the ore.

The depression of the 1930s brought an end to the Calumet & Arizona Mining Company through a merger with Phelps Dodge. During these same difficult years, rich ore bodies and very careful management allowed the mines of Bisbee to operate through troubling financial times, albeit at a much reduced level. World War II, by contrast, found Bisbee's mines in full production as part of the war effort. Lead and zinc had been produced as by-products of the copper operations for many years; now they were essential to the war effort and were mined as never before.

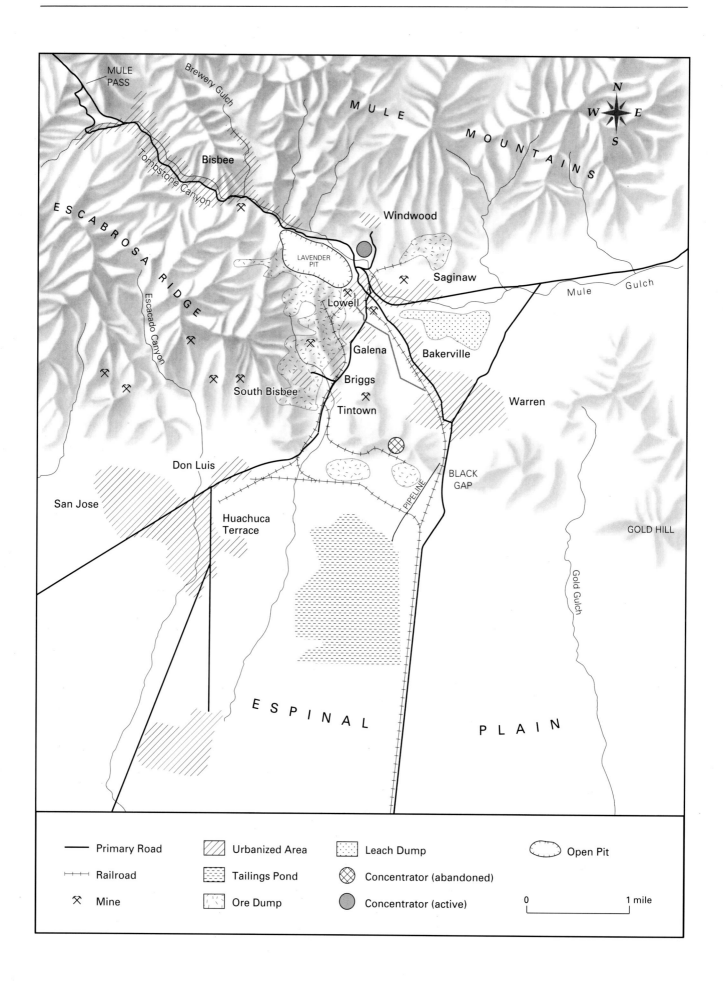

Primary Road

Railroad

Mine

Urbanized Area

Tailings Pond

Ore Dump

Leach Dump

Concentrator (abandoned)

Concentrator (active)

Open Pit

0   1 mile

Warren Mining District ca. 1974, showing Old Bisbee, Warren, and the Lavender Pit.

In 1951 work started on what was probably to be the last major development in Bisbee's mining history, the Lavender Pit. By 1954 ore was being processed by a new concentrator as it would be for the next twenty years. But late in 1974 the Lavender Pit reached its economic end, having moved 94 million tons of ore and 281 million tons of leach and waste. For a time the underground mines continued to produce copper from higher-grade ores as they had for nearly a century. Yet even these closed in mid-1975 when they were unable to bear the full burden of costs. Just as low-cost copper from mines of the western United States helped close high-cost operations in England and Michigan, so cheap copper from several foreign countries humbled the once great Copper Queen.

During nearly a century of copper mining, Bisbee produced a total of approximately 8 billion pounds of copper, 324 million pounds of lead, 355 million pounds of zinc, 28 million pounds of manganese, 102 million ounces of silver, and 2.8 million ounces of gold. Yet there remain millions of pounds of copper in the Mule Mountains, and the type of technological advance that earlier made low-grade materials into ore may yet find a way to mine these profitably. Perhaps another chapter of Bisbee's history as a mining center will be written. If so, it will be appropriate to say, "the Queen is dead; long live the Queen."

Bisbee's mining landscape as it appeared in the early 1980s. This photograph shows the headframe of the Campbell Shaft, Phelps Dodge's materials yard, and to the extreme right is a leaching operation designed to separate copper chemically from waste rock.

Everyday Life
in a Copper Camp

TOM VAUGHAN

At the confluence of two narrow canyons in Arizona's Mule Mountains, the settlement of Bisbee took shape at a deposit of copper discovered in the late 1870s. According to some of the first visitors to the site, the hills on either side of the canyon were thickly covered with oak, pinyon pine, and juniper. Once mining began, however, the trees were quickly cut down and the wood converted to fuel for mining works and cabin stoves. This dramatic alteration of the physical environment was typical of many changes that occurred in Bisbee between 1880 and 1920.

The first tent and cabin dwellings gave way to a commercial section composed of stores, saloons, hotels, and stables strung along the canyon floors. Business people struggled with the consequences of the community's remote location, the see-saw economy of mining, and the ravages of fires and floods.

As the population increased, residents gouged and blasted out hillside ledges for their homesites. Soon rows of houses perched one above the other until one neighbor's roof was just below another's front door. It was said that a "diligent housewife in the building above [could] step to the front porch and throw dishwater down her neighbor's stovepipe."[4] By 1900 the canyon bottom and most of the hillsides were crowded with buildings that housed as many as six thousand people. Long flights of almost vertical wooden stairs, winding dirt paths, twisting trails, and tortuous streets connected the mines, homes, and business sections.

A successful mining camp like Bisbee resembled a beehive alive with ceaseless movement. Men were lowered into shafts where around the clock they drilled, dynamited, mucked, and trammed the rock beneath the Mule Mountains. On the surface, the sights, sounds, and smells of ceaseless industry assaulted the senses. The din of rock crushers, explosions of dynamite, and the roar of the smelter competed with bellowing steam hoists and railway loco-

The flood of August 1908.

motives laboring to surmount the mountainous grade leading into Bisbee. A variety of acrid and pungent smells arose from a mixture of burned black powder, sulfurous smelter fumes, wood smoke, and animal and human excrement.

A Tucson newspaper reporter complained of Bisbee that "its vile odor is still in the nostrils when you have traveled far from the city."[5] Garbage littered the landscape and "nearly everything in the line of wearing apparel from hats to shoes" was strewn along the ravines waiting to be eaten by foraging animals or washed away during the summer rains.

Bisbee's population grew only slowly before 1900. Copper mining involved high capital, long-term investment, not the short boom-and-bust cycle typical of the gold and silver camps. So while its famous neighbor, Tombstone, mushroomed to a population of about eight thousand in a few years and then nearly died out, Bisbee remained well below that figure until after the turn of the century.

Bisbee's commercial district along Main Street was a mixture of wooden and brick structures in 1903. St. Elmo's Saloon, second building from the right, later moved to Brewery Gulch, where it remains today one of the few survivors of the dozens of drinking places that once lined the street.

Prospectors arrived first, men mainly from the American Midwest and East. They staked and filed claims, performed minimal assessment work, and enticed capitalists to invest in their properties. As copper production began, immigrants became a noticeable part of Bisbee's social make-up. The 1881 census reveals that more than half the population was foreign born, the majority being from Mexico, followed closely by those from the British Isles.

By 1900 more than one-third of Bisbee's residents were citizens of England, Ireland, Mexico, Finland, Austria, and Serbia. There were also many new arrivals from Italy, Germany, Sweden, and Switzerland. The organizations they formed included an Italian string band, a Finnish athletic club, a Cornish singing group, a German beer hall, and a Serbian benevolent society. Despite the wide variety of nationalities, northern Europeans and American-born whites dominated key aspects of Bisbee life.

As had happened in earlier conflagrations, the 1908 fire provided impetus for rebuilding and upgrading Bisbee's commercial district.

At all hours Bisbee streets were alive with people, some heading home at the close of a shift, others hurrying to work, or entering and leaving saloons, restaurants, and rooming houses.

In 1912 Serbian volunteers paraded down Brewery Gulch to the train station where they left to fight in the Balkan Wars.

Popular custom did not allow Chinese even to own businesses or spend the night in Bisbee. The *Bisbee Review* put it tersely in a 1903 article when the paper claimed that "an unwritten law has ever been strictly enforced, that no Chinaman would be allowed in camp. That law has never been violated."[6] Chinese did, however, live on farms along the nearby San Pedro River and deliver their produce to Bisbee, where the populace eagerly awaited their tasty vegetables.

Mexicans and Mexican Americans were typically hired only to work as surface laborers or in the smelter, not in the better paying underground jobs. The city of Bisbee paid Mexican laborers less than their white counterparts on municipal jobs, and local newspapers routinely used the term "Mexican" in a derogatory sense. For instance, one newspaper headline read, "Fatal Accident, Two Men Killed, J. H. Goodman and a Mexican Fall into Deep Sump." The article never mentioned the Mexican's name. Notwithstanding various forms of discrimination, Mexicans and Mexican Americans operated wood and water hauling businesses, restaurants, grocery stores, and other small enterprises. A few of them were professionals, such as dentists and court interpreters. Many put down roots in Bisbee by sending their children to school, and many purchased homes.

Bisbee's small Black community was discriminated against in a similar fashion. They were forced to attend segregated churches, denied access to fraternal organizations, and slurred and made fun of in the press. Nonetheless, they worked hard in the only jobs available to them as janitors, bootblacks, waiters, chauffeurs, and musicians. In the 1912 election local Blacks formed their own voting bloc.

Slovenians and other southern Europeans fared better than many immigrant groups, but they still suffered discrimination. J. B. Angius and V. G. Medigovich were business and political leaders of a group that thrived in the restaurant and grocery business, but by the end of the first decade of the twentieth century when Slavic immigration was at its height, popular feeling ran strongly against foreign-born workers. The Bisbee deportation of 1917 was as much an attack on immigrants as on the radical Industrial Workers of the World.

The role of wife and mother in all but the wealthiest circles was strenuous, difficult, and sometimes boring. The tasks of making, repairing, and cleaning clothes, caring for children, and cooking meals often involved more time than the eight hours a day a man typically worked in the mines. Added to that was a rigid social custom that discouraged women from entering many public places unaccompanied by a male.

Anna Crockett, above, *holds her baby, Harry, in front of the family home in 1899. This was a typical two-room cottage used by Bisbee miners.*

A Hispanic woman, right, *washes clothes in one of the Mule Mountain's seasonal watercourses.*

Lylaria Valenzuela Casillas, left, *ca. 1905, poses for a studio portrait. According to the federal census of 1910, approximately 5,500 Cochise County residents were born in Mexico.*

Maggie Letson posed for this formal family portrait ca. 1905. The Bisbee Review *observed upon her death in 1909: "Mrs. Letson was noted for her business acumen and at one time owned most of the property fronting on either side of Main Street. . . . Mrs. Letson numbered among her friends the substantial businessmen of the community and was well known for her business sagacity."*

The interior of the Orient Saloon on Main Street in 1904. Craps, faro, keno, poker, and roulette were available in a variety of saloons and betting was encouraged at most sporting events, including animal fights.

For the women of Bisbee, employment opportunities outside the home were limited mainly to sewing, teaching, and running boarding houses, hotels, and restaurants. Some found paying jobs as clerks in retail stores and shops and as waitresses. A few women owned commercial real estate, including saloons, but they found business difficult to conduct and often hired male agents to handle their public transactions.

As the copper camp developed, saloons dominated Bisbee's commercial district and formed the "nucleus of civilization," or so one local newspaperman claimed. The man's world of the saloon was almost plush with its mahogany and oak paneling and modern amenities like electric lights and telephones. In fact, the typical saloon functioned as a club where friends met, business deals were made, and men of like ethnic background congregated to socialize.

Saloons were also centers of vice. Most also functioned as gambling houses that attracted a "sporting fraternity" whose calling was to fleece miners of their pay, often with crooked methods. The combination of alcohol and gambling contributed to fights, killings, and suicides. One brawl, over the outcome of a poker game, ended in the dirt street outside and forced the resignation of a captain of the Arizona Rangers, a primary participant in the fracas. The general din and frenzy at the Bonanza Saloon was so great that nobody noticed until fourteen hours later that James Conner had put a bullet through his head. Another man lay dead of a heart attack for more than ten hours before any of the saloon habitués bothered to check on him. Clara Spaulding Brown, no doubt, spoke for many women when she observed in 1880 that "attractive saloons but accentuated the bare furnishings of the home and brought to mind the dreadful tragedies for which such enticing places are responsible."

Despite the controversy that surrounded them, saloons were extremely profitable business ventures that netted their owners thousands of dollars a month and provided jobs for a large force of men.

Most saloons never closed their doors but remained in tune with the twenty-four-hour workday of the mines. Saloon owners invested their abundant profits in local mining, real estate, and banking ventures. They were often generous to miners and prospectors, grubstaking them and later reaping rewards if a man struck pay dirt.

Women, except for prostitutes, did not frequent saloons. In fact, the first ordinance passed by Bisbee's newly appointed city council in February 1902 banned all women from saloons. The measure read in part that women were forbidden "in any saloon . . . , either for hire or otherwise, to sing, dance, recite, or play on any musical instrument, give any theatrical performance . . . , serve as waitress or barmaid, or take part . . . in any game of chance or amusement played in any saloon."

The law forbidding women in Bisbee saloons contained one major loop-hole: city fathers designated a red-light district in which women could engage in any of the above activities, and more. In fact, the city licensed and taxed the "bawdy houses" of Bisbee's red-light district, an area of cribs, whorehouses, dance halls, and saloons located on the upper end of Brewery Gulch. It was an area notorious for robbery, assault, and drug use.

Prostitutes were accurately described as "inmates" of the "cribs" that lined Brewery Gulch in this view ca. 1905.

Bisbee's mines employed neither women nor children underground. Some youngsters earned small sums delivering newspapers or hauling wood and water, but the abusive or blatantly exploitative forms of child labor found in the factories and mines of the East were uncommon in Bisbee. A boy poses with burros carrying firewood in 1905 in front of the home of William Brophy, manager of the Copper Queen store.

The prostitutes of Bisbee, for the most part, led lives of deprivation and scorn, were often addicted to alcohol and drugs, and died young. A few, especially "madams," invested in real estate and left the trade to marry or otherwise become respectable, but for the majority it was a wanton life in which they were shunned by decent folk, subject to abuse by male costumers and managers, and likely to be hauled repeatedly into court on a variety of misdemeanor charges.

A few respectable women did brave the forbidden doors of saloons, such as the three who entered the Bonanza Saloon one May evening in 1907 in search of their wayward husbands. When the three returned to the street they escorted "two big husky miners, one of whom was slightly under the influence of liquor, the other apparently sober." On another occasion a boarding-house proprietess entered the Shattuck Saloon on a Friday evening when the place was full and "verbally abused" a man sitting at a gambling table, claiming that he owed her money. "To avoid further embar-

Mrs. William Brophy sponsored one of the early communion classes held by Bisbee's Roman Catholic Church at the turn of the century.

Town children were encouraged, or at least permitted, to attend school until the eighth grade. Bisbee's elementary children, top right, *pose in front of their school in 1898. The present Central School building opened on this site in 1905.*

rassment he borrowed the money from friends and paid the bill." In yet another case, a Mrs. Mandeville entered the Orient Saloon when she heard that her son was gambling there, "and with a heavy whip lashed about her indiscriminately in front of the Faro table." The gamblers were relieved when mother and son left.[7]

The national wave of reform directed against crime, vice, and poverty swept through Bisbee in the early 1900s. The Bisbee Woman's Club was an active voice for reform, attacking the foul conditions of the city jail, lobbying for water fountains, horse troughs, and playgrounds, and instituting kindergarten in the public schools. The incorporation of the city in 1902 was the beginning of the end for the freewheeling saloons, gambling houses, and the red-light district. Gambling was outlawed in 1907, prostitution banned in 1910, and prohibition became law in Arizona in 1915.

While laws and social pressure were directed against crime and vice, a community of schools, churches, and social clubs was growing in Bisbee. The Copper Queen Consolidated Mining Company introduced vital community institutions such as a school (1883), library (1887), and company hospital (1890), three institutions that during the 1890s gave Bisbee a solid community foundation and an alternative to saloon life. The Copper Queen built the "Gymnasium Club" for its employees in 1904. It featured a gymnasium, shooting range, and later a hand-dug swimming pool.

It was during the early 1900s that a real proliferation of churches, schools, and community buildings occurred in Bisbee. The Meth-

The drum corps of Bisbee High School, bottom right, *poses prior to a football game with Clifton about 1910.*

odist Church (1900), Covenant Presbyterian Church (1903), and St. John's Episcopal Church (1904) were all constructed with some financial assistance from the Copper Queen Company. The Baptist Church was built in 1906, destroyed by fire in 1908, and rebuilt in 1909. A Black Baptist church was built on Chihuahua Hill in 1908. The Catholics constructed their first church in 1891, although it was segregated by 1904, and Mexican parishioners were forced to build a new Catholic church of their own on Chihuahua Hill.

By 1903 the public school had been rebuilt and enlarged almost yearly until it had become a hodgepodge of additions and an overcrowded mess. Bisbee's school superintendent began a bond drive to construct a new building in 1903. The ensuing campaign was notable in that women property owners were allowed to vote. The bond passed, Central School was built in 1905, and Bisbee's first high school graduation took place the following year.

In the 1880s adobe was a common building material, but with the coming of the railroad in 1889 lumber was more easily obtained. As a result, two- and three-room wood cottages became the domi-

These women, top right, enjoy the homelike facilities of the Young Women's Christian Association building constructed in 1912. The facility is still in operation in the 1990s.

The Copper Queen Company constructed a new hospital, bottom right, at the base of Sacramento Hill in 1902. The Colonial-style two-story structure had steam heat and the latest medical equipment. It could accommodate fifty patients.

The Finnish boarding house below was located in "Jiggerville" in 1912. The name of this neighborhood derives from the word "jigger," a Cornish term for cleaner of ores.

nant residential type in Bisbee. Houses were small by "back East" standards, and one visitor remarked: "Rents are high; even a two room unpainted shack, I am told, rents for $8 and $10 a month." Some men roomed together in a cabin or shack, but it was still expensive: a miner wrote home that "it costs so much to live here I never saw anything like it, one dollar a day for board alone." Miners with families rented or sometimes purchased the sparsely furnished cabins.[8]

The Copper Queen did not provide housing for miners in Bisbee, and so it is not surprising to find dozens of boarding houses, furnished rooms, and hotels in town by 1904. In spite of their number and almost continual additions, annexes, and new buildings, rooms remained difficult to obtain. One hotel proprietress stated: "I only wish I had one hundred more rooms for I could fill them every night. I have a continual stream of single men and men with families besieging me every day and night for rooms but I can not accommodate them."[9]

Apart from rent, other living expenses were high. Before pipes were installed, water was delivered in canvas bags on the backs of burros at a cost of fifty cents per bag. Wood was delivered the same way, and there was no electricity or indoor plumbing. Gardens could not be grown due to lack of water and space, and to the rocky soil.

The wealthy merchant and upper echelon company employee had larger and better furnished houses, but as one miner put it, "two rooms is considered a large house, the richest man's house here is

Bisbee's urban development was so haphazard that neighborhoods did not at first evolve into income-segregated patterns typical of more established urban centers. Many of the town's wealthy and influential families lived in Brewery Gulch along with poor and newly arrived immigrants. Walter Douglas's house, right, *featured terraced gardens but was juxtaposed with the less expensive houses of mine workers. The Douglas home began as a duplex adobe structure and was gentrified by various additions. He later moved to a new mansion in Warren, and this building was used as Bisbee's YWCA until the present structure was completed in 1912.*

Lemuel Shattuck opened a lumber business, below right, *in Brewery Gulch in 1899 and was quoted as saying that half the houses in town were built with wood from his yard.*

Adobe and sticks were used for Bisbee's cheapest housing.

as good as the poorest house in the east." Another newcomer commented, "The nice houses are simply bungalows and nobody has much room." Yet another stated that "he never saw a country with as much room out-of-doors and so little indoors."[10]

The better houses increasingly featured some of the amenities of the era: telephones, electricity, running water, and sewers. But in the 1890s many waste pipes still discharged "into the roads and gullies down which can be traced a saturated streak in some cases passing close to the neighboring houses."[11]

The layout of the planned suburb of Warren in 1906 and the opening of its trolley system in 1908 prepared the way for substantial houses and even mansions. Designed by the Calumet & Arizona Mining Company so that they could "retain the best class of employees," the company subdivided the land and sold lots. The fact that every lot was connected to sewers and electricity enabled the company to brag that it was "the most sanitary town in the country." Leading architects of the region, F. C. Hurst and Henry Trost, designed contemporary houses with appropriately large and landscaped yards.

The site of the earliest attempt to create an upper-class neighborhood was a plateau above Tombstone Canyon, across from Castle Rock, that became known as Quality Hill. There the Copper Queen Company built houses on mining claims for its management personnel, but the engineers and doctors who lived there could not compare its rocky, forlorn landscape to even a modest middle-class neighborhood back East.

Copper Queen employees lined up at the company office to collect their earnings (ca. 1915). Payday was a carnival-like time: drummers, peddlers, entertainers, gamblers, prostitutes, beggars, swindlers, and hoboes all converged on Bisbee to relieve the miners of their money on the tenth of each month.

The combination of the eight-hour workday, good and steady wages, and the tendency of miners to spend their earnings rapidly fostered almost limitless recreation and entertainment possibilities in Bisbee. That as early as 1889 the monthly payroll was sixty thousand dollars and that a captive audience of six hundred men was isolated in the Mule Mountains drew a variety of traveling performers to Bisbee.

Theater groups booked Bisbee on their cross-country tours, as one Tombstone newspaper writer observed in 1886: "Frush's Oriental Circus struck their tents this afternoon, and in the morning will take their departure for Bisbee." By 1897 the community had its own "opera house," containing "one of the best dance floors in the territory" and soon was attracting the "better class of traveling show." The *Tombstone Prospector* reported that in July of that year C. L. White gave Bisbee its first taste of moving pictures when he presented the Corbett-Fitzsimmons fight via his "Projectoscope."

By 1910 no less than four movie theaters were operating in Bisbee, featuring "up-to-date picture films, as well as full time orchestra and illustrated songs." The Orpheum Theater produced live performances from New York and Chicago, minstrel shows, Shakespeare, and wrestling. The Raymond Teal Musical Comedy Company was typical with "thirty people, dancing girls, and a carload of special scenery." There were the Quinn Brothers who sang an anvil song "while striking red hot sparks from a piece of steel heated to high temperature, producing a very pleasing effect in the darkened house."[12]

Mining companies often hired athletes, gave them light work, and thereby beefed up the local baseball team or gave the town a "World Champion" rock driller, as when Sell Tarr located in Bisbee. Boxing and wrestling thrived, although the former sometimes had to be staged south of the border in Mexico, where many Bisbeeites traveled anyway to watch bullfights. Those who could afford membership in the country club were welcome to play golf or tennis, though many preferred evenings of bridge. English residents of Bisbee imported soccer and cricket, while international rivalry was played out in tug-of-war contests such as the one in 1903 that pitted the Slovenians, Swedes, Irish, and the locals against one another for pride, prize money, and any bets that could be placed. D. A. Markey put a cool one thousand dollars on the Irish and doubled his money that evening.

This hard-rock drilling contest in 1902, right, drew thousands of spectators to Bisbee's town plaza on Main Street.

Dances were immensely popular, and just about any excuse to hold one was valid. People danced in parks, lodge halls, fire stations, and even mine headframes. For example, at the Spray Shaft in August 1900 "the magnificent steel gallows frame . . . was gaily decorated with hundreds of bunting . . . [and] from every bar and crosspiece of this gigantic structure swung thousands of Japanese lanterns." Pictured here is Warren's Labor Day dance in 1917.

Bisbee's steep slopes inspired a downhill coaster race that was held for the first time in 1911 and evolved into a popular annual event. Each entry had a crew of two: one to steer, a second person to brake on fast curves and push the coaster over rough spots. The race began at an elevation of over six thousand feet, followed a three-mile dirt course over bumps, holes, boulders, and trolley tracks to the finish line on Main Street, seven hundred feet below the start. The race was last staged in 1980 when two spectators were killed near the finish line.

A meeting of the Grand Commandery of Arizona Knights Templar was held in the Copper Queen Cave in 1897.

Fraternal organizations were the rage across the United States in the 1870s and 1880s, and Bisbee had its share. Although they appealed mainly to men, there were women's auxiliaries. Each had secret rituals, books, and costumes, marched in parades, organized memorial services, and held dances and fairs. They created a feeling of extended family, provided mutual aid in the form of sick and death benefits, generated business contacts, and were a source of political influence.

Bisbee's first lodge, installed in September 1883, was the Ancient Order of United Workmen. The Anglo-dominated fraternities such as Masons, Elks, Moose, Loyal Order of Redmen, Eagles, and Odd Fellows were the most powerful clubs politically and commercially. Mexicans and Mexican Americans organized La Allianza Hispano Americana and Blacks formed the Silver Leaf Club, although neither of these were listed in city directories nor were their events chronicled in local newspapers.

Bisbee celebrated holidays with gusto. Fourth of July, Memorial Day, and Washington's Birthday were welcomed with parades, sporting events, dances, and often fireworks and dynamite explosions. Foreign holidays were commemorated as well, often at the Pythian Castle where the member country's flag would fly over the building just below the Stars and Stripes. In 1912 the newspaper reported that more than half a dozen foreign flags had flown over the clock tower, attesting to the cosmopolitan make-up of Bisbee.

Though its growth was haphazard, Bisbee began to sort itself out into distinct districts after 1900. Main Street became the most desirable retail location, where rental space went for as much as $250 a month for a little shack in the heart of the saloon district in 1905 as compared to $150 for the best location within a large building in Tucson.

In Bisbee's retail district a person could find clothing stores, general merchandise, tailors, hotels, banks, and photography studios.

Customers were photographed in the French Kitchen Restaurant on Brewery Gulch in 1915. Restaurants abounded in Bisbee, many having distinctly ethnic names— English Kitchen, Edelweiss, and Vienna Bakery—but a visitor in 1900 remarked that "they would profit by a course at a cooking school." After the Copper Queen Hotel was built, a cook and staff were brought from California, and the elegant dining room modeled after a European plan.

The Fair Store began on Brewery Gulch in 1898, moved to Main Street the following year. It became a leading fashion house in Bisbee, a prominent general merchandise store known throughout Arizona Territory, and a wholesale supplier to stores throughout the Southwest. Brewery Gulch attracted many saloons, barbershops, cigar stores, variety stores, and wholesale meat and grocery businesses. Its streets were alive with pedestrians, horses, and wagons carrying groceries, meats, and fuel to other points of the city. The post office was located there for a few years but the constant congestion forced its removal to Main Street.

For the first twenty years of its existence Bisbee did not have a bank. Castaneda and Goldwater's safe was often used for the storage of valuables in the early 1880s, while the Copper Queen Mercantile took over that duty in later years of the century. It cashed checks and took deposits from cattlemen and others from the outlying districts of Arizona and Mexico.

Horse-drawn vehicles once competed for space on Bisbee's crowded and dusty streets: there were laundry, bakery, grocery, ice, and milk wagons, as well as the stagecoaches that linked Bisbee and outlying towns, and every form of personal conveyance.

At the south end of Brewery Gulch, two "automobilists" pose with their prize possessions ca. 1907. Note that the steering wheel is located on the right side of each vehicle. Doctors, lawyers, judges, and mining company officials were the usual owners. They often hired chauffeurs, as was the case with the automobile on the right.

Real banking got its start when the Bank of Bisbee opened its doors in 1900, and by the end of that decade the Miners and Merchants, Citizens, and First National all had buildings on Main Street—although the First National failed in 1909 because of the unsavory lending and investing practices of its president. Despite such setbacks, Bisbee became the center of commercial and banking activities for the mining and cattle industries of southern Arizona and northern Sonora, Mexico. It was where supplies could be purchased or ordered, loans secured, and deposits made. There was a continuous flow of cattlemen, capitalists, and mining men in and out of Bisbee.

Until the arrival of the trolley in 1908, most residents walked, or on occasion rented a buggy. There was little room to keep a riding animal and feed was expensive, as was boarding at a livery stable. Nonetheless, traffic became so thick that in 1906 a traffic jam occurred: "About 5 o'clock wagons and buggies coming from all directions met in the lower end of Brewery Avenue and for ten minutes none of them could move."[15]

Runaways were inevitable, as in 1898 when the horses of a wagon containing empty beer kegs suddenly bolted, scattering the cargo of the wagon everywhere. A Mrs. Garland was killed and her husband seriously injured when they were thrown from their buggy after their horse ran away while they were driving down a steep grade. Two prostitutes made things quite lively in July 1906 when they decided to stage an impromptu horse race in Brewery Gulch: they were stopped, jailed, and fined for disturbing the peace.

Automobiles began appearing on Bisbee streets as early as 1900 when the *Bisbee Review* reported: "A real live automobile has arrived in Bisbee and has attracted much attention." But for several more years the new invention was rarely seen on town streets, and certainly it was not transportation for the common person.

Bisbee's history between 1898 and 1917 was one of transition from a mining camp to industrial mining city. It was an exciting period of change during which the population grew from about four thousand to twenty-five thousand. Wooden buildings of the late nineties gave

Town growth constantly altered the appearance of Main Street, as here in 1906 when numerous buildings were being renovated and the old post office had come down in preparation for building a new one.

way to the more permanent brick, block, and concrete structures of the early 1900s. Horseback and horse-drawn conveyances were predominant forms of transportation during the first part of this period, but by its end, trolley cars and automobiles were competing for space on the narrow streets. The sturdy burros, bearers of water and wood for so many years, were turned loose to roam the hillsides, and modern utilities such as piped-in gas, water, electricity, and telephones reached all points of the city.

It was a time when trains arrived four or five times a day, when capitalists came to invest in mining properties, when hundreds of businesses thrived in Brewery Gulch, on Main Street, and in Lowell. During those years more than twenty mining development companies sunk millions of dollars into the underground prospects. The monthly payroll of the two largest companies, the Copper Queen and Calumet & Arizona, swelled to more than $1 million.

The boom was so intense that major fires failed to slow its momentum. On the night of October 12, 1908, a fire roared through the Main Street business district, destroying most of that two-block section, including many houses. Rebuilding began immediately and within two years all the commercial buildings were in place, this time constructed of brick and concrete throughout.

World War I and the deportation of 1917 ended Bisbee's exuberant period of growth and excitement. When Cochise County Sheriff Harry Wheeler forced more than a thousand miners into freight cars to be carried to the New Mexico desert, he removed the radical labor element but also the dominance of the unmarried tramp miner. The family orientated, company-dominated town was firmly in place.

A hose cart race in 1907 sought to polish firefighters' skills. Men from all the mines participated during important holidays. This preparation did not prevent the great fire of 1908, which destroyed much of Bisbee's commercial district.

Making Connections

DON L. HOFSOMMER

Bisbee and the Railroads of the Southwest

DON L. HOFSOMMER

Proud railroaders pose with Arizona and South Eastern engine number 1 in Bisbee ca. 1895.

Basic details concerning the origins, development, and construction of the West's transcontinental railroads are readily available in any good American history text. Less well known and understood is the process of fleshing out a nationwide rail network through construction of numerous branch lines. Feeders were built for a variety of reasons: to connect areas bypassed by trunk roads with the outside world; to haul logs, coal, or other specific commodities; or, to guard an established service area against potential intrusion by a competing railroad company. In still other cases, shippers themselves instituted rail service when they perceived that established carriers failed to meet their needs. The case of Bisbee includes several of these variables.

Located away from what became the Southern Pacific's (SP) "Sunset Route," Bisbee's introduction to railroad-made America took place within the context of surging demand for copper. During the decade of the 1880s mines in the future states of Montana, Utah, and Arizona were opened to satisfy an insatiable appetite for the copper products required to electrify the nation's homes and businesses.

In Montana the focus was on Butte, which one geologist hailed as the most important mining center in the United States. The tracks of a predecessor of the Union Pacific Railway first reached the Butte mining district in 1881; the Montana Union Railroad—owned jointly by the Union Pacific and the Northern Pacific—soon followed; and, a predecessor of the Great Northern penetrated the area in 1889. Not satisfied with this assortment of competing carriers, the Anaconda Company formed its own railroad in 1892, the Butte, Anaconda & Pacific, which linked mines at Butte with the smelter at Anaconda, twenty-six miles west.

The mining of copper in Utah began somewhat earlier and, like the Montana experience, was characterized by a mix of common carrier operations provided by a single producer—in this case the Utah Copper Company, later Kennecott. When the Denver & Rio Grande failed to maintain an important branch, Utah Copper built its own road from the Bingham mines, southwest of Salt Lake City, to the reduction plant at Garfield.

In Arizona, the mining of copper centered on Globe, Jerome, Clifton, Morenci, and Bisbee—none of which was located on rail thoroughfares. The Jerome area drew a narrow gauge road and a predecessor of the Atchison, Topeka & Santa Fe (Santa Fe), while the others were served by lines that were eventually owned by the Southern Pacific.

Arizona's overall development might have been otherwise. The Santa Fe took an early interest in the southeastern corner of the territory, and with its eye on a Pacific outlet at Guaymas, Mexico, thrust a line from Benson through Fairbank to Nogales in 1882 using its subsidiary company, the New Mexico & Arizona Railroad. This route missed both Tombstone and Bisbee whose representatives were given short shrift when they approached Santa Fe officials in favor of their respective communities. Santa Fe's haughty attitude was not quickly forgotten by locals who, because the towns remained devoid of rail service, were forced to move freight to distant railheads by teams of eighteen to twenty mules or horses.

While hardly a booming metropolis, Bisbee in 1882 boasted a number of stores, a hotel, and—more importantly—copper mines and a smelter. Phelps, Dodge & Company acquired property in and about the region and consolidated those interests in 1885 to form a subsidiary, the Copper Queen Consolidated Mining Company. Except for the lack of modern and efficient transportation opportunities, the future of Bisbee looked good. Stagecoach operators easily handled a swelling volume of passengers, but the process of shipping freight by wagon remained expensive and frustrating. What was required, all hands agreed, was direct rail service.

To that end, the Copper Queen fostered incorporation of the Arizona & South Eastern Rail Road Company on May 24, 1888. Its raison d'etre was clear enough: to link Bisbee with the outside world via the Santa Fe's New Mexico & Arizona line. To the great satisfaction of Copper Queen boosters and other locals, this thirty-six-mile line triumphantly entered service in February 1, 1889. The new link cost more than $450,000 to build, but the cost of moving freight was reduced by a ratio of six to one. The little Arizona & South Eastern Rail Road earned so much money that it retired its mortgage debt in a matter of months.

The new railroad had a predictably impressive impact on Bisbee. As the Copper Queen prospered, so did the community. And by any measure the Copper Queen was doing exceedingly well. In 1887 it

Stagecoaches once transported passengers from the nearest railhead at Fairbank to Tombstone and Bisbee. A railway line reached Bisbee at last in 1889 but did not reach Tombstone until 1903.

Transportation of various types figured prominently in Bisbee's history. Burros provided a sure-footed means to haul building materials up the town's steep hillsides. The photo is ca. 1906.

In the 1880s the Copper Queen experimented with a steam traction engine called "Geronimo" to move tonnage from Bisbee to Fairbank. It ran well enough in the dry season but did poorly in the rain, and it required that a great quantity of wood be stacked at intervals for refueling along the road. According to legend, it gave operators more trouble than the Apache leader Geronimo, and hence the name.

Laying the first tracks into Bisbee in 1889. The white frame building was the town's library. The stone building became the Copper Queen Mercantile store.

introduced the use of electricity to serve lighting needs within certain of its facilities; it expanded service to the railroad's roundhouse and depot in 1889, and to the company store and the town's library four years later. Electrification represented progress and prosperity.

The outside world increasingly took note of this remote place. There was no choice. The demand for copper continued its dramatic upward spiral even as reserves of high-grade ore from Michigan's famed Keweenaw Peninsula proved inadequate to meet growing demand. The arrival in Bisbee on October 15, 1899, of a special train bearing members of the American Institute of Mining Engineers said it all. They had inspected mining operations in Montana, Oregon, Washington, and California; Bisbee was their final stop. The symbolism was perfect. Just as Montana had surpassed Michigan in the production of copper during 1887, so would Arizona in 1910 surpass Montana to take first place in United States production. Bisbee was affected most directly. The population increased to more than seven thousand in 1900, and would reach twenty-five thousand in 1919. Bisbee was no longer a mining camp; it was a mining center. The twin engines of change were the onrushing industrial revolution with copper as a key metal in the process and a rapidly maturing rail network that offered reliable and efficient transportation to all parts of the country.

Yet the path of change was uneven. For instance, traditional veins played out and the Copper Queen failed to acquire potential reserves that were snapped up by well-known mining personalities from Michigan who would presently afford stout competition to the Phelps Dodge subsidiary. That hardly meant that the Copper Queen would vacate the field. Indeed, it committed to a program of revitalizing mining operations at Bisbee by way of mass-production techniques to exploit low-grade, finely disseminated ore while at the same time adopting a froth flotation process to derive concentrates. There was, however, one remaining matter of concern: the need for additional rail outlets to afford competition while at the same time expanding route options.

Relations between the Copper Queen and its Arizona & South Eastern on the one hand, and the Santa Fe and its New Mexico & Arizona on the other, were never better than crusty. The breaking point was at hand when Arizona & South Eastern representatives asked the Santa Fe for an adjustment of rates via Fairbank and were told that the Santa Fe was not running the New Mexico & Arizona for the benefit of the Copper Queen. Senior management at Phelps Dodge displayed no sense of humor when told of this and quickly dispatched a civil engineer to canvass the territory between Fairbank—the Arizona & South Eastern's end-of-track—and Benson, same twenty miles distant on the Southern Pacific. Developments moved quickly. The new extension was placed in service late in 1894. Traffic patterns continued to reflect the importance of the copper industry: for every ton of copper outbound, between one and two tons of bituminous coal and about two tons of coke moved to Bisbee.

Additional plans for railroad expansion surfaced shortly thereafter when Phelps Dodge acquired a copper mine at Nacozari, Mexico, nearly one hundred miles southeast of Bisbee. A short branch soon extended across the Espinal Plain to the new village of Naco. Its construction implied the start of a direct line to Nacozari and rumor had Phelps Dodge constructing a smelter near Naco to handle concentrate from both Bisbee and Nacozari.

Events proved somewhat otherwise. Another location was chosen for the smelter—about twenty miles east of Bisbee where land was available at reasonable prices, where an adequate supply of water was readily at hand, and to which point rails could be extended from Bisbee on the west and from Nacozari on the south. Construction began during the summer of 1900 on the line from Bisbee to the new townsite of Douglas.

A mixed freight and passenger train of the Arizona and South Eastern Rail Road pauses along the San Pedro River two miles south of Charleston in the summer of 1890.

The railroad landscape in Bisbee ca. 1890.
This photograph shows the railway yards, a
two-stall roundhouse, and a turntable.

Meanwhile, Phelps Dodge found the Southern Pacific no more sympathetic to its needs than the Santa Fe had been. Not long after the Copper Queen's Arizona & South Eastern reached Benson, the Santa Fe sold its New Mexico & Arizona branch to the Southern Pacific. Thus once again the Arizona & South Eastern was dependent on a sole connecting carrier. Then, too, there was the very configuration of the Arizona & South Eastern which offered at best an indirect route for inbound materials that were billed almost exclusively from the east. A new outlet, one to the east, would remedy that problem.

Phelps Dodge personnel approached the Southern Pacific with the suggestion that it build a branch southwestward to or, at least, in the direction of Douglas from its main line at or near Lordsburg, New Mexico. SP managers no doubt recognized that such a line would reduce transit time and in that way benefit the Copper

Queen. But construction of such a route would be, from SP's point of view, duplicative. It would add appreciable capital and operating costs without compensating benefit since SP was already handling the business over its existing line to Benson and no addition in point-to-point revenue could be expected if the new line were, in fact, constructed. Small wonder that SP would have none of the proposal.

Phelps Dodge, however, saw the matter in darker terms. Indeed, Phelps Dodge and its Copper Queen subsidiary would teach the obdurate Southern Pacific a lesson in the proper treatment of important customers. To that end, papers were filed on October 19, 1900, to incorporate the Southwestern Railroad of Arizona, which pledged to build a line to the eastern boundary of Arizona, ostensibly from Douglas. Phelps Dodge was obviously seeking competitive connections, but there were few options: the Santa Fe at Deming or El Paso, the Texas & Pacific at El Paso, the Southern Pacific at El Paso or at some location to the west thereof, or the Chicago, Rock Island & Pacific, if it should extend its line southwestward from Kansas to Texas or New Mexico.

Meanwhile, rails reached Douglas from near Bisbee in February 1901, and graders proceeded to the northeast. On June 1, Phelps Dodge announced that Deming was its target destination. At that location connection could be made with the Southern Pacific and, ironically, given its earlier experience, with the Santa Fe. The first train operated over the 155-mile line from Douglas through Hachita to Deming on February 13, 1902. Still not content, Phelps Dodge ordered another route from Hermanas, on the Douglas-Deming line, to El Paso. This one entered service in December 1902. Collaterally, the name of the Southwestern Railroad of Arizona was changed to the El Paso & Southwestern Railroad (EP&SW), and shortly thereafter the Arizona & South Eastern was sold to the new company.*

The El Paso & Southwestern, or "Sunshine Line" as it styled itself, took title to another five hundred miles of track extending in a northeasterly direction from El Paso to a very important connection with the Chicago, Rock Island & Pacific (CRI&P or Rock Island). A branch from Tucumcari to Dawson in northern New Mexico reached coal mines acquired by Phelps Dodge.

*The El Paso and Southwestern was not owned directly by Phelps, Dodge & Company but rather, along with other rail subsidiaries, by the El Paso & Southwestern Company. The stock of this holding company was held by the principal owners of Phelps Dodge, viz. Arthur Curtiss James and associates, C. H. Dodge and associates, the Douglas family, and four smaller parties. That Phelps Dodge controlled the EP&SW, however, is not in question.

A map of the El Paso & Southwestern System on the eve of World War I. Courtesy: University of Arizona Special Collections

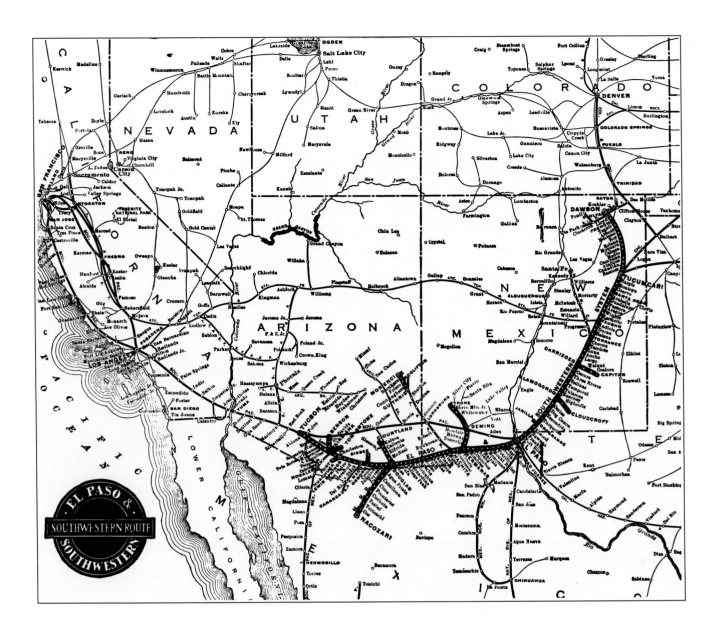

Thus, in a very brief time, the fledgling rail operations of the Copper Queen had grown to significance. Now the El Paso & Southwestern offered its customers optional routings to and from the East, although its sole western connection remained the Southern Pacific at Fairbank and Benson.

Aspirations for the new smelter town of Douglas quickly came to flower. Not only were plans going forward on the part of Copper Queen but, in addition, the Calumet & Arizona Mining Company announced plans for a smelter at Douglas and, in fact, its furnace was blown in on November 15, 1902. The larger smelter built by Copper Queen came on line during the spring of 1904. Douglas grew accordingly. Saloons dotted the landscape, the town boasted five hotels, and some people correctly forecast a new street railway.

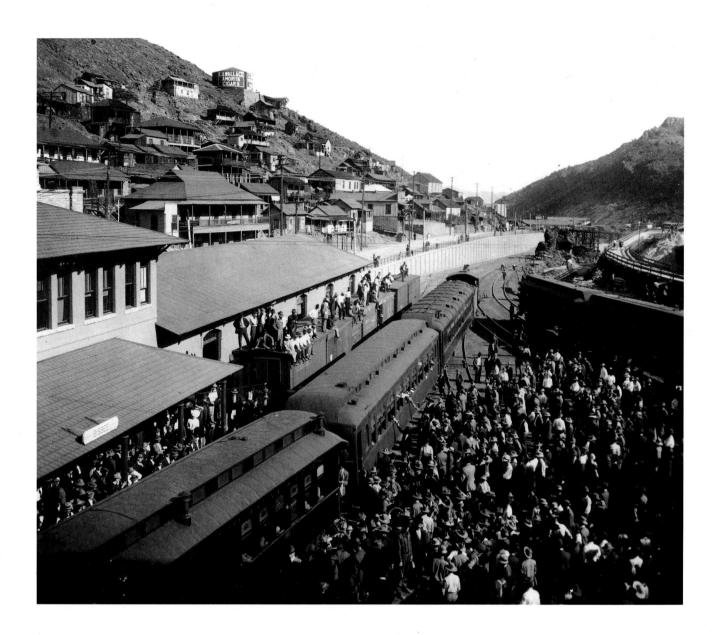

These several developments had an impact on Bisbee. Smelting there ended during the summer of 1904, although mining operations continued to expand. In terms of rail service, through trains ceased making their side trips to Bisbee and, instead, the EP&SW instituted local connecting service by way of Osborn (Bisbee Junction). None of this implied that Bisbee had fallen on hard times. In fact, growing economic activity meant that the town's tiny rail yard was frequently "plugged." In the narrow canyon, streets, houses, mining apparatus, the railroad itself, and drainage requirements took up all available space and precluded expansion of the EP&SW's facilities. Shippers were left to grumble and shift as best they could. They were especially vexed to learn that in many cases their cars were stalled just outside of town awaiting a chance to enter the crowded rail yard.

Well-wishers gather at Bisbee's El Paso &
Southwestern station in 1912 as Serbian vol-
unteers begin their trek to Europe to fight
in the latest Balkan War. The depot, located
a short distance east of the Copper Queen
office building, was torn down in 1950.

The El Paso & Southwestern served well the purposes of Phelps Dodge and its other customers and, in the process, made money in its own right. Traffic mirrored the constantly growing demand for copper. Small wonder that the great trunk roads looked covetously on the prosperous regional carrier. Edward H. Harriman, for example, never hid his interest in procuring the EP&SW for the Southern Pacific. But managers of Phelps Dodge displayed no interest in selling.

On the other hand, they recognized that the EP&SW had distinct limitations. It was tied ever so directly to a narrow traffic base. If the copper industry prospered, so too would the railroad; if copper stumbled, so too would the EP&SW. In addition, its limited route structure—essentially starting nowhere and ending nowhere—would prove a tremendous liability if copper business turned downward. To militate against these problems, Phelps Dodge through its EP&SW in 1910 acquired a sizable holding in the Rock Island line to protect and anchor its eastern flank. In the same year, EP&SW managers placed in the field a number of engineers who were ordered to seek a logical route westward from Benson. What was their goal? Was it Tucson or perhaps even Los Angeles? There were many at Phelps Dodge and at the EP&SW who dreamed of reaching the Pacific Coast, but for now they had to settle for less. Rails from Benson reached Tucson on October 31, 1912.

With a 772-mile, dipper-shaped route extending from Tucumcari to Tucson (the portion from Tucumcari to Santa Rosa was owned by the Rock Island and leased to the EP&SW) and with an impressive holding in Rock Island, EP&SW managers began a calculated campaign to attract through or overhead freight traffic to hedge against fluctuations in local business. The Rock Island was perfectly willing to cooperate, especially since Tucumcari gave that road its maximum haul on transcontinental business. Not surprisingly, the Southern Pacific looked unfavorably on the prospect since its participation would be scaled back to business only west of Tucson. Neither did the Santa Fe look with favor on the prospect. Nevertheless, the EP&SW prevailed and its properties were upgraded to handle the new business.

Passenger service was also altered. To this point such service could best be described as "local." Dramatic changes came in 1913 when the crack Golden State Limited from Chicago to Los Angeles was routed over EP&SW tracks between El Paso and Tucson. Connecting service to Bisbee was offered by way of Osborn so that in 1916, for example, a traveler could leave Bisbee at 6:15 A.M. and be in El Paso at 1:40 P.M., in Kansas City at 7:10 P.M. the following day, or in Chicago at 10:15 A.M. the second day. Westbound, passengers could leave Bisbee at 9:05 P.M., arrive in Tucson at 12:26 A.M., and

be in Los Angeles at 2:30 P.M. the following day. Additional service was by a "make all stations" local in each direction plus five daily shuttles between Bisbee and Osborn via Lowell and Don Luis. Express on the EP&SW was handled by Wells Fargo & Company.

The best expectations for the EP&SW were realized during World War I when loadings of copper soared; its worst fears were realized in the postwar slump. With traffic volumes and operating revenues down, Phelps Dodge in the early 1920s reexamined its position regarding the railroad. Again company officials looked longingly to the west and for ways to extend the EP&SW from Tucson to tidewater—this, of course, as a means of gathering longer hauls and greater revenues. Terminal property was acquired in Los Angeles and this move predictably fueled rumors that the EP&SW would build a line parallel to the Southern Pacific between Tucson and the West Coast.

Summertime excursions took picnickers to Lewis Springs on the San Pedro River. With its shade trees and water, the area was one of Bisbee's popular recreation spots. A more distant vacation retreat was the cool mountaintop resort town of Cloudcroft, New Mexico, which was located near the El Paso & Southwestern main line.

Events proved otherwise. The Southern Pacific, in a clearly ex-
pansionistic mood following resolution of a lengthy and encumbering legal matter in 1923, quietly sent emissaries to Phelps Dodge.
The following June, an agreement was reached whereby the Southern Pacific acquired the EP&SW by issuing stocks and bonds to EP&SW
equity holders and by assuming the EP&SW debt. The contract was
effective November 1, 1924.

The matter required approval by the Interstate Commerce Commission, but that was not a problem since there was general public
support for the acquisition, since SP could productively integrate the
EP&SW into its route structure, and since the regulatory body had
already recommended inclusion of the EP&SW into the SP under the

*The number of transfer wagons lined up in
the shade of the Copper Queen store testifies
to the important role the railroad played in
Bisbee life. Seen here in 1903, the wagons
transported commercial goods and passengers' trunks and suitcases to and from the El
Paso & Southwestern depot.*

Transportation Act of 1920. The deal was significant in its scope and in its ramifications; in a sense, it presaged the great rail mergers of recent decades.

The Southern Pacific did mold the former EP&SW into its operating plan. Much of the line between Benson and Tucson—better engineered than the SP route—became a second main track and enjoyed heavy usage. The line from El Paso to Tucumcari took on even greater importance as the SP affirmed allegiance to the Rock Island over the "Golden State Route." Indeed, virtually all of the former EP&SW remained of value through the prosperous 1920s.

That was not the case during the grim days of the 1930s. Hard times claimed the Calumet & Arizona Mining Company whose properties passed into Phelps Dodge hands in 1931. Arizona remained the nation's number one state in terms of copper production, though in 1932 the state's smelters turned out only 201 million pounds. The Southern Pacific was forced to take a hard look at all operations and, to be sure, nearly foundered in a sea of red ink. In Arizona it trimmed branches and determined to use the line between Douglas and El Paso only for certain passenger trains and as a "safety valve" in case trouble blocked the Sunset Route between El Paso and Tucson.

Prosperity for the copper industry and for the nation at large returned with World War II and continued into the postwar era. Smelter production declined after 1943, but mine production continued with Arizona still leading all states. Change was in the offing, nevertheless. The railroad industry in the postwar era was subject to severe modal competition—for freight and passengers alike—and dieselization and other technological improvements allowed for longer and fewer trains, lessening demand for capacity. The result was significant reduction in track miles. Arizona was not immune. In 1961, the Southern Pacific terminated operations east of Douglas to just west of El Paso, 209 miles, on the old El Paso & Southwestern line. The track is now gone, but the cinder-coated right-of-way, several impressive concrete culverts, and a weathered water tank at Hermanas remain plainly visible from New Mexico Highway 9.

The railroad did not give life to Bisbee as it did to countless other communities in the American West. Rather, it was the area's rich mineral resource base that attracted the rails, and it was dissatisfaction with trunk roads that propelled the major shipper into the side business of rail carriage. This scenario was not unique to Bisbee, but it was unusual, and the size of the El Paso & Southwestern and the ultimate scope of its operation make the story quite remarkable.

That the EP&SW passed to ownership of a larger carrier is in the classic pattern of railroads that had either to expand or expire; and, the EP&SW experience is a case study in the merger movement that has been such an important element in the history of American railroads. That much of the EP&SW trackage has disappeared also reflects the industry standard.

So, while the railroad did not yield life to Bisbee, the connection it provided to the outside world certainly molded and nurtured many facets of community and economic life in a remote corner of the Southwest. Railroads, after all, represented the most modern transportation device available just when the great mineral deposits of Bisbee became a most desirable element in the industrial revolution. No surprise, then, that Bisbee and the railroad would grow up together.

"The Finest Mine on Earth"

CLARK C. SPENCE

Western Mine Promotion and Investment

In most areas of the West, early mining methods and milling processes varied little. They were simple, individualistic techniques calling for a low input of capital and a high input of labor. Generally, the first discoveries were of placer gold, easily handled by the classical but inefficient modes of panning, the use of "cradles" or sluice-boxes. Free milling quartz found in outcrops on or near the surface could readily be crushed with a stamp mill and the gold separated with mercury, again with a high loss of precious metal. But the day of these elementary techniques was short. In most regions free milling ore was scarce and gold-bearing gravels of the streams were worked out quickly, often within a year or two. Miners then followed the outcroppings deep into the ground, with capital requirements mounting.

Tunneling and shafting were expensive, and blasting was costly as well as dangerous. Expensive power drills soon replaced simple ones operated by hand. Heavy expenditures were required for ventilation, for moving the ore underground and hoisting it to the surface. In addition, hundreds of thousands of board-feet of timber went to shore up mine interiors. By 1881, for example, the deeper shafts of Nevada's Comstock Lode extended down three thousand feet, and the total length of underground workings and interconnections was somewhere between 180 and 190 miles, all timber-supported. Bisbee's Copper Queen Mine required thirty board-feet of timber for each of the eight hundred tons of ore extracted every day in 1904 (or a total of twenty-four thousand board-feet of timber each working day). A veritable underground forest lined its passageways. Clearly, deep-level mining was big business.

Advancing technology made mining even bigger business. With time and place, the nature of ores changed so that the standard process of separation no longer worked. Chlorination, introduced into California gold fields at the end of the fifties, and Washoe pan

This photograph shows miners and a pneumatic drill, with which two men could complete enough holes for a blast in half a shift. Working by hand, it took two skilled men two shifts to drill the number of holes required for blasting.

amalgamation, developed on the Comstock a few years later, functioned reasonably well but were wasteful. But in many other parts
of the West, ores were more complex, with silver as well as gold
often in combination with sulfur or base metals. Such "rebellious"
ores did not respond to the normal milling procedures and evoked
trial-and-error experimentation based on everything except scientific principles. Eastern "experts" in 1870 introduced fantastic new
approaches like the "Improved-back-action-lightning-gum-elastic-
cylinder-and-Spanish-fly amalgamator" which promised to "*draw
gold from a Rocky Mountain turnip.*"[14]

This "process mania," combined with rampant speculation in
both mines and mills, brought a sharp mining depression in 1864,
which left thousands of investors with shattered dreams and the
western landscape with rusting abandoned machinery. Only when
a remarkable group of metallurgists, many of them European-born
and German-trained, solved the riddle of complex ores, did mining respond positively. The Canadian-born James Douglas helped
develop a process to deal effectively with complex gold and copper
ores well before he made his mark on Bisbee.

These solutions, like hard-rock, deep-level mining, required a
heavy outlay of capital. So did the new "mass production" techniques introduced from time to time. Hydraulic mining depended
on diverting streams of water, to be dropped through pipes, then
shot through a nozzle under tremendous pressure to literally wash
away the sides of mountains to be run through long sluices where
the gold was separated. At the end of the century, gold dredging was
another innovation: a self-contained digging unit floated on its own
hull, scooped up gravel, processed it for gold, and dumped the tailings in an unsightly ridge as it moved slowly forward over land that
may have been worked once or even twice before by hand. About
the same time came the introduction of the low-grade copper techniques based on the processing of immense amounts of dirt by huge
machines in smelters and refineries much larger than any hereto-
fore used. All these were revolutionary, took a good deal of the risk
out of mining, and required vast inputs of capital. Throughout the
mining West, simple mining, sustained by blister-and-callous labor,
gave way to high-capital corporate mining. In Bisbee the processing
of ore involved ever more sophisticated and expensive technology.
The most dramatic of these changes was the new Copper Queen
smelter erected in nearby Douglas at a cost of $2.5 million.

Western mining has always been built on unbounded faith. Corporate mining broadened the base of that faith, adding to that of
prospectors and discoverers, that of promoters, capitalists, investors,
and speculators. In the early mining camp, every man was a poten-

*Miners pose at the entrance to an uniden-
tified mine. The scene could be anywhere
in the West and was typical of the labor-
intensive first stage of underground mining.*

tial millionaire. Every pocket was full of samples from the Bobtail Horse, the Let-Her-Rip or the Root-Hog-or-Die, each one undeveloped, but "the greatest mine on earth, Suh!" even though the owner owed the grocer and had no credit anywhere in town.

When companies took over, new importance was assumed by the mine promoter, that imaginative and persistent midwife in the transfer of property to a corporation with capital. Eternally optimistic and not always burdened down with scruples, the mine promoter was defined by one critic as "a man who has unlimited capital behind him but not any in front of him; his watch is in soak." Often these "barefooted capitalists," as editors called them, were not held in high repute.[15]

Promoters come, promoters go
    But mostly, soon or late,
They leave a load of waste and woe,
    A heritage of hate.[16]

But, taken as a group—good and bad alike—they were vital in the transition from a Western mining frontier to a Western mining industry. For every fast-talking cheat puffing up a worthless wildcat ledge into an Arabian Knight's treasure trove for the profit to be made from promotion itself, there was another seeking to interest capital for legitimate development of promising property. And for every investor willing to take a "flyer" on a get-rich-quick scheme, there was another who was much more cautious and informed when he bought mining stock.

Promoters were a dime a dozen and included professionals like William J. Sutherland, described as "expansive and expensive, florid and flamboyant, persuasive and persistent,"[17] and English-born Whitaker Wright—a veteran of the Leadville, Colorado, boom and a millionaire by the age of thirty-three—who ultimately stood trial for swindling the public but terminated proceedings by swallowing a cocktail of potassium cyanide. Among them were reputable mining engineers like the Barringer brothers, who tried to organize a firm to exploit commercially a giant meteor believed embedded in Meteor Crater in Arizona, but who had a somewhat jaundiced view of mine owners in that part of the world. "You have to deal with them differently from what you would with an honest man (the honest man is a rarity anyway, especially in the southwest),"[18] one of them wrote in 1896.

Many a Western politician tried his hand at mine promotion, among them three different territorial governors of Arizona, including John C. Fremont, whose talented wife, Jessie, proved more adept at the art than he. The ranks of promoters also included amateurs like Charles Moore, who ran the Alturas Hotel and several restaurants in Hailey, Idaho, and crossed the Atlantic eight times to promote Wood River property; and the Reverend Calvin A. Pogue, who played a mean guitar in Tombstone and who floated several Arizona mining companies in the 1870s with investments from other clergymen and their flocks. ("A Saintly Syndicate," sneered a skeptical editor. "Presbyterian Preachers in a prodigious Pool." "They Stir Up the Arizona Wildcat with the Gospel Rake, and He Scampereth Like Samson's Foxes."[19]

Normally, the promoter did not purchase mining property outright. He merely "bonded" it; that is, he took an option to buy at an agreed-upon price before some specified date, three or four months or perhaps as long as a year hence. During that time, he tried to attract capitalists at whatever profit the market would bear. One Nevada promoter offered gold property he had under option for $32,000 for a cool $1 million; another acquired rights to a Colorado mine for $45,000 and proposed organizing a New York company to take it over for $5 million.

George Warren is often mistakenly identified as the discoverer of the Copper Queen claim. In fact, he owned only one-ninth of the property, which he lost on a bet that he could outrun a horse. He died penniless and insane. In this formal portrait by C. S. Fly, Warren poses amidst the supposed tools of a pioneer Arizona prospector-miner. The pick is actually a studio prop, probably used by railroad workers rather than miners.

Once obtaining an option, the promoter brought in a few friends to help organize a company, tried to bribe well-known public figures with free stock to sit on the board, obtained comments from "leading mining experts" (often on the same basis), and headed for San Francisco or Manhattan with an elaborate prospectus to solicit capital. Promoter Edward Reilly "bonded" Bisbee's Copper Queen Mine for $20,000 and then found San Francisco investors willing to put up the actual capital with Reilly reaping a reward of half interest in the mine for his salesmanship.

In Britain, prospectuses included the names of titled "guinea pigs" (paid a guinea per board meeting) to catch the eye of "the lord-loving public," as one critic phrased it in 1872,[20] but in the United States the names of politicians were almost as good. In 1882, for example, the Silver Mesa Mining Company, with property near Durango, Colorado, boasted among its directors a general, a former secretary of the treasury, and two United States senators.

Any good prospectus taxed the imagination. That of the Pyramid Range Silver Mountain Company, Ltd., soliciting investment in a New Mexico mine in 1871, reached a new high in creative fiction. Even one of those connected with it later admitted that it "put the tales of Baron Munchausen in the shade."[21] Estimates of future profits were generous, sometimes even fantastic, if one believed prospectuses. "Enormous dividends" were promised; fifty percent earnings immediately; a hundred dollars invested would re-

A bearded Dr. James Douglas, together with Ben Williams, far left, prepare to take visitors into a mine. The occasion may have been the 1899 national convention of mining engineers in Bisbee.

turn "from THIRTY TO ONE HUNDRED DOLLARS PER YEAR, AND UPWARDS."[22] Undeveloped mines were often represented in the late nineteenth century as extensions of fabulously rich lodes and were invariably "true fissure veins," which became even richer the deeper they went—a truism known by everyone except geologists and engineers.

Numerous Colorado prospectuses of the 1860s cited a letter of assayer Edward Kent that "Colorado is destined, in my opinion, to rival or supersede California and Australia, and become the Eldorado of the West." In the same fashion, writers of Nevada prospectuses were fond of quoting Methodist Bishop Matthew Simpson ("one of the purest and most intelligent men of his age"), who told an audience in the New York Academy of Music in 1864 that Nevada had enough silver to pay off the national debt, even if it went to $20 billion, and to give every returning soldier a musket of silver and to replate the Union ironclads with the same precious metal.[23]

At the same time, prospectuses sought to link their properties with well-known paying operations. A Colorado mining directory of 1879 listed seven Comstock, six Homestake, five Potosi, and two Gould and Curry mines, each a rich property elsewhere, yet unknown in Colorado. No Nevada prospectus was complete without a glowing statistical survey of silver production on the Comstock, even though the property being pushed was in Humboldt or Austin, halfway across the state. The peak of richness by association and of readers' ignorance of geography was reached in the prospectus of the Old Guard Mining Company, Ltd. (1887), which observed that the firm's property in Arizona was about the same size as that of the successful Drumlummon mine and looked even more promising. Not a word was said to indicate that the Drumlummon was not "just down the road a piece," but was in Montana, about a thousand miles away.

Prospectuses usually had positive statements by "mining experts," though knowledgeable people warned that "mining speculation, like transactions in horse-flesh, have a tendency to blunt the moral perspectives," and that local citizens testifying on the good points of a mining proposition sometimes turned out to have an interest or to be "saloon loafers" who did so "for the nominal consideration of so many fingers of whisky."[24] Sometimes, the promoter put rich ore samples on display. In the early eighties it was charged that both a Colorado and a New Mexico mining company, neighbors in a New York office building, used the same ore samples—taken from a Utah mine! Thus any serious buyer or large-scale investor sent out his own examining engineer to take independent samplings and assays. Phelps, Dodge & Company sent James Douglas to Arizona in 1881 to provide it accurate information on copper prospects. Even

Components of mine development: technology, money, and know-how. Walter Douglas stands second from the right.

so, the salting of mine property or the doctoring of the samples of the expert was not an uncommon occurrence, and enough of it was successful that companies in all parts of the mining West were occasionally fleeced.

One such fleecing took place in 1907 when the Bisbee Copper Company tried to raise more than a million dollars in London by telling investors that its mine property was near both the Copper Queen and Calumet & Arizona operations and that the manager of the Copper Queen was its president. None of this was true. Simple exaggeration rather than outright lying was more common, as when Captain B. W. Tibby publicly stated that he had made the Mascot Mine near Bisbee "famous" and claimed to have found some of the largest copper mines in the country. Neither of his boasts can be substantiated.

On the whole, however, Western mining was based on legitimate investment and optimistic but not promotional puffery or fraudulent appraisals. The combination of plain-dealing promoters and knowledgeable capitalists who calculated their risks carefully was always strong enough to sustain the industry. In 1903 a trainload of Michigan investors came to Bisbee to look over mining prospects, specifically various properties of Calumet & Arizona, which had a Michigan connection. Bisbee mining stock at that time generated a "fever of excitement" in Michigan, but these would-be investors wanted to verify the claims of promoters.

Much of the capital was generated within the United States, from the East Coast, the Midwest, or San Francisco. And much of it was plowed back from profitable mine or mill operations. Dotted here and there were concerns like the Mining Company Nederland in Colorado, a Dutch firm with some Czarist Russian capital or the Société Anoynme des Mines de Lexington, a French outfit operating in both Utah and Montana. More obvious were several hundred British joint-stock companies, which in the last forty years of the nineteenth century invested as much as $50 million in Western mines, apart from California. But the bulk of capital was American. Of the deep-level companies surveyed in 1880 and of 632 registered or incorporated in Colorado fifteen years later, roughly 98 percent were American-owned.

A large group of capitalists inspects copper properties in northern Mexico. They include Arizona mine promoter Colonel W. C. Green and would-be investors William G. Rockefeller and Edward H. Harriman.

Like prospecting, mine investment and speculation became a virus. During one Idaho boom in the 1860s, gold nuggets grew in people's imagination, as one contemporary put it, "like asparagus in a hot bed."[25] Wild manipulation by insiders at home or among the curbstone brokers of San Francisco might cause violent fluctuations on the market and create both fortunes and paupers over the course of a few weeks or few days. Shares of the Alpha mine on the Comstock, for example, were bulled to $1,570 in February 1868, but had plunged to $33 by September of the same year. Promoter-speculators like Stephen Roberts noted in 1878 that mining was a gamble at best and "there is no harm in letting the public take some of the chances. . . . We will play our hand so that the public cannot see whether we hold aces or deuces, but if they guess aces, so much the better for us."[26]

Dabblers bought low-priced stock in "outside mines"—a synonym for "wildcat." They bought "on margin," paying part of the value down and borrowing the rest from the broker, only to have to cough up more cash if the shares went down and the broker called for "more mud" to make good. The Chinese, too, played the mining market, acting as their own brokers, and were substantial holders in Nevada mines and were subsequently burned in Idaho stocks like everybody else. In the late seventies a Presbyterian minister in San Francisco was compelled to leave his calling for one in which he could make a living after his church had gone heavily into debt because of mining stock manipulation. A Campbellite church at Woodland, west of Sacramento, was also stung in a wildcat stock scheme involving the Excelsior in Globe District, Arizona. In Bisbee the president of the First National Bank of Bisbee went to prison in 1909 for secretly using his investors' funds for personal mining speculation, and the bank collapsed as well.

Investors came from all walks of life and from most parts of the country but especially from middle-sized and large cities. Manhattan was one of the centers for Western "mining men and schemers," as well as for heavy capitalists who sometimes "get the mining fever bad," as one engineer put it.[27] Just after the turn of the century, an agent for a Goldfield, Nevada, brokerage firm lamented the general hard-going in mine stock sales in Philadelphia and blamed history: "It is not one man in 1000 that has not lost money in some mine out West," he said in 1905.[28] A West Coast editor in 1862 believed that there was more San Francisco capital invested in Nevada's Washoe silver than in all the gold mines of California; another estimated thirteen years later that about fifty thousand people in the City by the Golden Gate were directly or indirectly interested in mining stocks. "The market extends everywhere," noted an editor during the Comstock craze of the 1860s.[29]

The Czar Shaft of the Copper Queen was located southeast of Bisbee, which is visible beyond the stacks. This photograph shows both the mine timbers used underground and the slag dump for the smelter. The date is approximately 1890.

Investors in Western mining properties included the famous as well as the little people. They included boarding-house owners in Virginia City, Salvation Army personnel in Houston, traveling salesmen who bought goldfield stock from the owner of the Pacific Hotel in Norfolk, Nebraska. They included politicians like Vice President Garret Hobart and Senators James G. Blaine, Benjamin F. Butler, and Preston Plumb, who was supposed to have cleared $3 million in two years from his mining investments. Territorial governors Lew Wallace of New Mexico, F. A. Tritle of Arizona, and Samuel Houser of Montana were all owners of mining stock.

Industrialist Samuel Colt, inventor of the revolver, had important holdings in Arizona; Marshall Field, the Chicago mercantile king, was a major owner of the Chrysolite at Leadville. Cyrus McCormick, manufacturer of farm implements, had many mineral investments, including the Reaper Mine near Tucson. Other familiar names among mine investors included novelist Owen Wister, poet Walt Whitman, artist Albert Bierstadt, women's rights advocate Carrie Chapman Catt, orator Robert G. Ingersoll, and generals George B. McClellan, Ulysses S. Grant, and Daniel Sickles.

In the dark interior of the Copper Queen smelter ca. 1890, workers pose with thimble carts as they pour out slag to be hauled to the dump.

Showman Buffalo Bill Cody poured considerable money into an Arizona mine; Ned Buntline, the publicist who gave Cody his start, owned shares in a Black Hills company, while John M. Burke, business manager of Buffalo Bill's Wild West show, had holdings in Colorado. A professional baseball team, the Detroit Tigers, invested in the Bisbee Extension Mine.

Whether many of these investors reaped much profit is doubtful. Some did, but the real money was to be made by the shrewd entrepreneurs with the ability to judge men and mines and with access to capital when opportunity arose. These were generally neither run-of-the-mill investors nor the original discoverers of property. There were always exceptions like Lemuel "Sandy" Bowers, who struck it rich on the Comstock and eventually ran the full cycle back to poverty.

Every camp had its rags to riches success story, as when Martin Costello bought Bisbee's Irish Mag property for $1800 and sold it in 1899 for $500,000. But in far more instances the discoverers sold out for a pittance to men who subsequently made millions out of the property. Henry T. P. Comstock sold his portion of the lode that bore his name for $11,000 and two jackasses, beasts which in terms of later yield cost him $1.5 million each. Comstock died in 1870, a penniless suicide. At Butte, that "island of easy money completely surrounded by whiskey," old Bill Parka struck an incredibly rich vein of copper ore but sold out for a mere $10,000, then settled back to watch the new owners take a million dollars from that "richest hill on earth."

The real winners were men like the Guggenheim brothers, whose sphere was global; James Douglas, Daniel Jackling, and William A. Clark, who built Western copper empires; or the California triumvirate of George Hearst, James Ben Ali Haggin, and Lloyd Tevis, who controlled more than a hundred mines, among them the rich Homestake, Anaconda, and Ontario. They and their ilk—the Marcus Dalys, the Samuel Newhouses, the Frederick Bradleys, the Bernard Baruchs—were among the most fortunate. They had good advice and were excellent judges of both people and prospects.

A dramatic night view of slag being dumped at the new Copper Queen smelter in Douglas ca. 1904.

Toil and Trouble

CARLOS A. SCHWANTES

Rhythms of Work Life

Work in Bisbee and many other parts of the West in the early twentieth century had a peculiarly regional quality about it. Certain aspects of mining were the same regardless of locality, yet distinct patterns and rhythms set work life in the West apart from that in major industrial centers of the East and Midwest. Two key concepts that explain much about Western labor are the dispersed and isolated nature of its population centers and the concentration of its work force in natural-resource based industries plagued by recurrent bouts of cyclical and seasonal unemployment.

A slump in the price of copper might close dozens of mines across the West from Bisbee to Butte and send hundreds, even thousands, of miners off in search of work in other camps and even in other industries, such as logging and agriculture. In some ways the job seekers were no different from the unemployed of Chicago, New York, or Boston, who upon losing one job might trudge down the street in search of another. Their counterparts in the West, however, tended to be more visible because the loss of a job in one of the region's natural resource-based communities often meant having to travel across vast empty spaces to another island of settlement, usually some distance away, to find work.

Every Western mining community had its homebody and tramp miners, the latter typically being young, single, and restless men who drifted from job to job. From Arizona the tramp miners typically migrated north in summer to jobs in Utah, Nevada, and Montana, and south again in winter. The mining companies of Bisbee actively recruited married men, not tramp miners, apparently in the belief that this created a more stable community of workers. Sixty-five percent of Copper Queen employees in 1917 had been on the job longer than a year; yet it is even more significant that another fifteen percent had been employed for less than one month. Rates of annual labor turnover averaging one-quarter of the total work

Two miners pose in their work clothes in the photographic studio of O. L. Dowe about 1904.

force were common in western copper mines. The United States secretary of labor worried in 1918 that so large a pool of migratory labor might develop a sense of injustice and serve as "inflammable material for beguiling agitators to work upon."[30]

The racial and ethnic composition of Bisbee's mine labor was ever changing. In the early years the vast majority of skilled miners were American-born whites. Most learned their trade in the mines of the West. As production of copper increased toward the end of the nineteenth century, so too did the demand for labor. While the majority of miners in Bisbee remained American-born whites, Northern European immigrants began to arrive in noticeable numbers. Many came from the mines of Cumberland and Cornwall, England, and from Scotland, Germany, and Ireland. They brought with them skills learned in the mines of their homelands.

Still another change occurred with the increased mechanization of the mineral industry in the early twentieth century. Technological innovations reduced the level of skill required for many jobs. Consequently, it became possible—even desirable from the perspective of management in a highly competitive industry—for mining companies to reduce their labor costs by hiring replacement workers who were less-skilled and thus lower-paid. Mines and smelters of the West soon came to depend heavily on unskilled and semi-skilled immigrant labor from Southern and Eastern Europe. Bisbee now became home to a variety of new ethnic groups.

As in other Western mining towns, a system of informal residential and job segregation evolved. American-born whites and Northern Europeans were usually on one side, and Eastern and Southern Europeans on the other. Forming still a third distinct group were the Hispanics who tended to reside on Chihuahua Hill, a section of town apparently named for a Mexican state, and in Tintown. Mexicans and Mexican Americans were usually relegated to less prestigious and lower paying jobs, such as mucking and tramming underground, although in some places prejudice and custom did not even permit them below ground. In early twentieth-century Arizona, even organized labor supported a variety of laws hostile to Hispanic workers.

Nearly all mine foremen, engineers, and mechanics were native-born whites or immigrants from Northern and Western Europe. Forming something of a labor aristocracy were the numerous English miners from Cornwall. Mining in that county dated from as early as 1580, but copper and tin went into a slump in the 1860s and as many as one-third of the men left for mining frontiers of the New World.

A group of miners poses in D. A. Markey's studio (ca. 1895) with their lunch buckets and candles. The flecks of white on their shirts and pants are actually droplets of wax from their candles, which indicates that they have just come from work. If the miners were Cornish or Finnish, their lunch buckets probably carried soup in the lower portion and pasties in the top.

Muckers and trammers needed less skill, and these jobs went mostly to Finns, Italians, Serbians, and Montenegrans who were paid correspondingly lower wages. Mexicans were predominantly surface laborers and paid still less. Wages in 1910 ranged from $1.25 a day for Mexicans, Mexican Americans, and Italians to $3.50 for native-born whites and northern and western Europeans, although such differences related as much to levels of skill as to race and ethnicity. In fact, the two were impossible to separate.

Encouraging Mexicans to seek jobs in Arizona was the revolution that wracked their country from 1910 to 1920 and the recently completed railroad lines that facilitated travel from interior Mexico to the northern border. Especially after Bisbee's infamous deportation of July 1917, the number of Hispanics in the local work force increased dramatically, with some of them moving even into skilled positions. On the Copper Queen payroll the following August were

2,104 people, of whom 369 were Mexicans. Although most of them worked in the newly opened Sacramento Pit, another 44 worked underground. None, however, served as foremen or bosses. Hispanics were not common in the mines of other states, especially as one moved north from the border; they nonetheless played a significant role in the history of Bisbee.

Women did not hold jobs in mines, except for the few who worked as secretaries and stenographers in company offices. To be sure, women could be found in any mining camp, though not in large numbers at first. A few arrived as wives, others to manage rooming houses and eating places. An unknown number worked as prostitutes in places like Brewery Gulch.

Over the years mining technology changed, and so did labor requirements in the mines—from reliance on hand-held drills to pneumatic ones. Conversion from underground to open-pit operations likewise sped up production even as it decreased the need for traditional mining skills. Superseding candles as a source of illumination in the mines were carbide lights, which were in turn replaced by electric storage battery models. Even with such advances, underground mining remained a dangerous business, although the mines of Bisbee were safer than most. In fact, the main threat to a miner's health came from disease. The Copper Queen reported in 1904 that typhoid fever that year accounted for 10,322 days lost from production.

Governor George W. P. Hunt, third from the right, relaxes in the lobby of Brewery Gulch's Victoria Hotel. Seen here in the mid-1920s, he served a total of seven terms as governor, though his early friendliness toward organized labor was gone by the time he returned to office in 1923.

Women switchboard operators ("Hello Girls") manually routed calls, probably at the Bisbee Improvement Company, around the time of the First World War.

In the early twentieth century, Arizona was considered a strong-
hold of organized labor. George W. P. Hunt, a Democrat friendly to
labor, presided over the 1910 Constitutional Convention, and labor
played a major role in writing the resulting document, though it
did not receive all the provisions it sought. After statehood, Hunt
served as governor of Arizona from 1912 to 1916 and continued to
be known for his fair treatment of organized labor.

Bisbee had nine unions in 1916, which encompassed a variety
of trades, from bootblacks, cooks, and bakers to meat cutters, bar-
bers, and carpenters. There was a local of the Western Federation
of Miners, although the union had a difficult time maintaining a
presence in the mines. In the early twentieth century all three of

Bisbee's major mining companies adhered to the principle of the open shop. The Copper Queen, moreover, paid better than union scale wages and carefully observed the eight-hour day mandated by an Arizona law that took effect on June 1, 1903.

When an organizer from the Western Federation of Miners came to town in 1906, Bisbee miners voted 2,888 to 428 against joining the union. At that time the average miner received $3.50 a day, 50 cents higher than the union scale. The copper companies nonetheless took no chances and dismissed four hundred miners believed to have union leanings.

In early 1907 the Western Federation renewed its effort to organize Bisbee miners, who had apparently become restive because of recent introduction of modern equipment that required a less skilled work force underground. The companies' response was to lay off eight hundred men, ostensibly because of a shortage of fuel for smelters and the need to make repairs in the mines. By early April

Meat cutting was one of several trades unionized in pre–World War I Bisbee.

some sixteen hundred men were out of work as copper companies continued to flex their muscles to discourage union activity. The result was Bisbee's first mining strike when three thousand men walked out.

Copper companies fired and blacklisted strikers and hired replacements, mostly Mexicans, and this inevitably increased ethnic tensions in Bisbee. After ten months of strife, the Western Federation called off the bitter affair and Bisbee once again became a non-union camp. The fact that 1907 was a recession year combined with the importation of strike breakers crippled union labor. For the next decade the Bisbee mines remained non-union. But World War I gave rise to conditions that favored renewed efforts to organize Bisbee's miners.

War greatly increased the demand for copper, which was used in munitions and communications equipment. Every rifle cartridge, for example, contained about half an ounce of pure copper. As a result, copper prices climbed dramatically, from 26.5 cents a pound in the summer of 1916 to 37 cents a pound the following March. The cost of living increased, too, and wages did not keep pace. Some miners left for better paying jobs elsewhere. Those who stayed behind produced at a hectic pace, with successive shifts working around the clock. Labor grew discontented.

Into this situation stepped two competing unions. The more moderate organization was the International Union of Mine Mill and Smelter Workers, successor (in 1916) to the old Western Federation of Miners and an affiliate of the American Federation of Labor. Much farther left was the Metal Mine Workers Industrial Union No. 800, an affiliate of the radical Industrial Workers of the World (IWW).

In mid-May 1917 members of the IWW captured the Bisbee local of the Mine Mill union. They drew up a list of grievances and presented these on June 26 to Gerald Sherman, mine superintendent at the Copper Queen. He responded by tearing them up. Infuriated by Sherman's response, local IWW leaders called a strike without benefit of the vote of the Bisbee membership. Probably no more than 400 miners out of Bisbee's 4,700 mine workers actually paid dues to the IWW, and many of those were also members of the Mine Mill union. Nonetheless, approximately 3,000 miners walked out on June 27.

The strike dragged on for two weeks. It remained peaceable, although tensions rose with each passing day. Public attention increasingly focused on the radical program of Industrial Workers of the World rather than on the specific demands of mine workers. On July 3, Charles Moyer, head of the Mine Mill Union, wired Arizona

governor Thomas E. Campbell that the Bisbee local was a maverick and the strike unauthorized. Three days later Moyer revoked the charter of the Bisbee local and called for workers to ignore iww picket lines.

Even in the best of times the iww frightened employers with its radical program and its reputation for violent confrontation, and clearly the first few months of the Great War were not the best of times. Wobblies (as members of the iww were popularly known) were now widely regarded as agents of enemy Germany. Many people in Bisbee were aware that the iww had recently published several pamphlets advocating sabotage as a means of bringing about sweeping social and economic changes.

Linked to the fear of Wobblies, sabotage, and German subversion was growing concern about Mexican revolutionaries. Bisbee was a border community, and the Mexican Revolution had been part of its consciousness for several years. Battles had been fought

In this turn-of-the-century view, smelter workers pose next to the Copper Queen's huge converters. The ingots of molten copper will cool and harden, and from Bisbee they will likely go to a refinery in El Paso.

Bisbee had a front row seat for the Mexican revolution. Using children in armed conflicts is nothing new: this boy posed among a group of well-armed adults in Naco, Sonora, in 1913. From the relative safety of the United States side, American tourists watched pitched battles only a short distance away. A Bisbee Daily Review *article on the 1913 siege of Naco reported: "There were hundreds of Kodaks [small cameras] among the visitors of the day and on both sides of the line many photographs were taken."*

on its doorstep in Naco, Sonora, both in 1913 and 1915. Even more ominous, however, was the example of another border community, Columbus, New Mexico, where in March 1916 a predawn raid by Pancho Villa's rebel troops caught people unprepared. The Villistas torched buildings and killed seventeen Americans.

There can be no doubt that unease in Bisbee was linked to anti-Mexican feeling. Cochise County Sheriff Harry Wheeler claimed as much when he expressed fear that idle Mexican workers gathered in Douglas might run amok. Phelps Dodge, however, played down the anti-Mexican threat because it employed so many Hispanics. How many of the rumors that swept through Bisbee in mid-1917 were part of a cynical attempt to discredit the IWW and how many were sincerely believed is hard to know now.

In any case, a portent of what would happen in Bisbee occurred on July 10 when vigilantes in the copper camp of Jerome, about three hundred miles northwest of Bisbee, deported sixty-seven "troublemakers" alleged to be members of the IWW. Two days later Bisbee's winding streets echoed with the footsteps of a posse comitatus that was two thousand men strong. Armed with a previously prepared list of names, they carried out a deportation of a size and scope unprecedented in American history.

To ensure their success, the conspirators allowed no messages to leave Bisbee. Their leader was Cochise County Sheriff Wheeler, and backing him were local mining companies that had combined to organize a Workman's Loyalty League and a Bisbee Citizens Protective League. The two bands of armed vigilantes were reminiscent of the Western frontier.

Men identified only by white arm bands raided the houses of known strikers and sympathizers, including some lawyers, tradesmen, and businessmen, who were taken into custody. A deputy seeking to arrest a member of the IWW was killed; his assailant was slain, in turn, by a fellow deputy. These were the only deaths to occur during the violent round-up of approximately two thousand men.

The "undesirables" were taken first to the downtown plaza and then to the ball park in Warren where mine company officials offered each prisoner a last chance to return to work. Some did. The remaining men were then marched between two lines of armed citizens to a special freight train provided by the Phelps Dodge–controlled railroad, the El Paso & Southwestern.

The train rattled east across the desert toward Columbus, New Mexico, 174 miles away. When officials there would not permit the unusual cargo to be unloaded, the train stopped at Hermanas where the deportees were simply abandoned. A nearby army camp supplied them with water, their first in twelve hours. Food sent by

Violence of various types and vigilantism were nothing new to southeastern Arizona in 1917. An earlier example was that of John Heath hanged in Tombstone in 1884 by enraged Bisbee residents. He was the ringleader of a failed robbery attempt in Bisbee in which five innocent bystanders died. When the court failed to sentence him to death, a mob from Bisbee broke into the Tombstone jail and hanged Heath from a nearby pole. The coroner listed the apparent cause of death as asphyxiation.

A well-armed Lieutenant Johnny Brooks, right, of the Arizona Rangers poses for a formal portrait. When the Arizona Rangers was formed in 1901, Bisbee was its first headquarters. Rangers broke strikes at Morenci and Globe and earned a reputation as an anti-labor force. The territory disbanded them in 1909, ostensibly as an economy move. Ironically, when Harry Wheeler was a Ranger captain during Bisbee's 1907 strike, organized labor credited him with preventing company thugs from intimidating protesting workers.

the United States government from El Paso reached the men by nightfall. The following day a troop of soldiers escorted them to Columbus, where the federal government maintained a camp for the deportees until mid-September.

A census taken by the United States Army on August 5 revealed that of the 1,003 men who remained in the refugee camp, 804 were foreign-born. Of these, 530 were aliens. Twenty different nationalities were represented among the foreign born, with the largest number of deportees being Mexicans (268) followed by Austro-Hungarians (179) and British (149).

A long line of prisoners and their captors marched through Lowell on July 12, 1917.

Deportees, below left, *were loaded aboard El Paso & Southwestern freight cars at Warren. An armed deputy identified by his white arm band appears to prod reluctant prisoners aboard a cattle car.*

A total of 1,186 men were shipped out of Warren in twenty-three cattle- and boxcars, each of which held an average of 50 men. Near Columbus, New Mexico, they would be dumped out of the cars onto a desiccated and seemingly endless expanse of creosote bush, spiny yucca, and stunted mesquite.

The deportees briefly considered returning en masse to Bisbee, but that meant a ten- to fifteen-day hike through desolate desert terrain where daytime temperatures hovered around one hundred degrees. They also considered commandeering a train in an effort to force action by federal officials. In fact, most deportees quietly slipped away during the next several weeks and never returned to Bisbee.

It should be noted that Bisbee was not alone in giving vent to IWW hostility. The Wobblies' unorthodox forms of protest had landed hundreds of them in jail in Spokane, Washington, and led to violence in the California cities of Fresno and San Diego. In the sawmill town of Everett, Washington, several people died in a violent confrontation between Wobblies and lawmen in November 1916. Butte vigilantes lynched IWW organizer Frank Little only a few days after the Bisbee deportation. On September 5, 1917, the United States government's agents simultaneously raided Wobbly halls across the country and placed many leaders under arrest.

What most distinguished the Bisbee deportation was the number of people involved and the fact it had the approval of both business leaders and law enforcement officials. The latter were no doubt somewhat surprised by public hostility to the deportation. Since the early days of the mining frontier in California, banishment had

been a common way of dealing with individuals who were perceived as trouble makers. On several occasions in the early twentieth century the state of Colorado had banished union miners to Kansas and New Mexico. Miners even practiced banishment themselves, as happened in Telluride, Colorado, and Goldfield, Nevada, during the first decade of the new century.

President Woodrow Wilson's Mediation Commission went to Arizona to investigate the trouble. Following hearings in Phoenix, Globe, Clifton, and Bisbee, it published a report that branded deportation as "wholly illegal and without authority in law, either State or Federal." Members emphasized its harmful effects on the war effort. A federal grand jury indicted Sheriff Wheeler and twenty Bisbee mining, business, and professional men in 1918 for violating the rights of the deportees, but a federal district court invalidated the indictment, a decision upheld on appeal to the United States Supreme Court, which said the matter should be decided by Arizona courts. The federal judiciary found that participants in the deportation had acted out of "the law of necessity."

The state of Arizona arraigned 210 Bisbee citizens, including Sheriff Wheeler. One case was tried in the spring of 1920, but acquittal on the first ballot led to dismissal of criminal charges against all other defendants. As a result almost all plaintiffs in the civil damage suits that totaled more than six million dollars dropped their cases, although a few claims were settled out of court for small sums.

Copper companies agreed not to discriminate against Mine Mill members after the deportation, yet they refused to tolerate more militant and independent unions. With encouragement from the companies, Mexicans took the jobs of many former strikers, and joining them was a new type of laborer—young men from agricultural and mining districts of the Midwest. The union was beaten. For more than a decade the miners of Arizona remained virtually unorganized.

Today, many people who know nothing else about Bisbee have some vague notion of the deportation. It often rates at least a line or two in college American history textbooks. Regardless of one's view of the still controversial episode, it is best recalled as part of the larger rhythms of life in Bisbee, especially during the war year 1917, when a series of unsettling events combined to bring down the curtain on the community's "age of innocence."

During the years between 1880 and 1920, Bisbee evolved from mining camp to aspiring Arizona metropolis. For nearly a century it remained a major center of copper production in the United States. Bisbee's remarkable built environment now preserves that era of American history better than any of its peer communities can. Bing-

The open-pit mining of Sacramento Hill began a new era in Bisbee's industrial history. In the foreground, tailings encroach upon the houses of Jiggerville in December 1918.

ham in Utah, for instance, is now gone, gobbled up by the open-pit mine that once gave it life. Butte, Montana, was a lively producer of copper, too, and still has the look of mining about it. Headframes and mine dumps dot the landscape, and the enormous Berkeley Pit east of town is a landmark comparable to Bisbee's Lavender Pit. Although the old commercial heart of Butte still dominates the surrounding landscape from its hilltop location, the town in many ways seems tired; and perhaps because of the ordinariness of the grid pattern of its principal streets, Butte has a look not much different from that of any other gritty urban-industrial center in America.

Certainly my bias is clear here, but one of Bisbee's many charms is that its older streets retain the eccentric layout typical of early mining camps, and its original business and residential districts are cradled by copper-hued hills that remind a visitor of the town's main reason for existence. The work of building Bisbee during the formative decades before 1917 remains visible for all to see, on the pages of this book as well as in the community itself.

Notes

1. James Douglas, unpublished memoirs, 1909, Phelps Dodge Corporation files.

2. James Douglas, unpublished speech, 1912, Phelps Dodge Corporation files.

3. James Douglas, unpublished memoirs, 1909, Phelps Dodge Corporation files.

4. Frank Aley, "Bisbee, Arizona's Premier Copper Mining Camp," *Pacific Coast Miner*, April 18, 1903, p. 1.

5. As quoted in M. Elizabeth Cole, *Jottings from Overland Trip to Arizona and California* (privately published 1908), p. 23.

6. *Bisbee Daily Review*, July 31, 1903.

7. *Bisbee Daily Review*, December 2, 1905.

8. Letters of Fred Hickory, Bisbee Mining and Historical Museum.

9. *Bisbee Daily Review*, November 25, 1903.

10. Letters of Frank Hall, July 18, 1913, Bisbee Mining and Historical Museum.

11. Report of Frederick W. Farquhar, November 27, 1896, City Records in Bisbee Mining and Historical Museum.

12. *Bisbee Daily Review*, July 26, 1907; February 11, 1908; February 15, 1910.

13. *Bisbee Daily Review*, April 11, 1906.

14. *The Rocky Mountain Directory and Colorado Gazetteer, For 1871* (Denver, 1870), p. 245.

15. *Idaho Tri-Weekly Statesman*, May 28 and November 1, 1881; *Mining and Scientific Press*, 79 (September 2, 1899), p. 257.

16. From "Promoters," by J. C. Murray, in Eugene Louis Chicanot, comp. and ed., *Rhymes of the Miner* (Gardenvale, n. d.), p. 129.

17. Thomas A. Richard, *A History of American Mining* (New York, 1932), p. 68; Sidney Lee, et al., eds., *Dictionary of National Biography* (London, 1901–1949), Suppl. 2, III, pp. 711–13.

18. Lewin Barringer to Daniel M. Barringer (February 11, 1896), copy, Daniel M. Barringer MSS, Princeton University.

19. *San Francisco Chronicle*, November 19, 1877; Reports on the Mines of the Aztec Mining District, Santa Rita Mountains, Arizona Territory, October, 1877 (San Francisco, 1877), pp. 1, 2–3, 5–6.

20. *Mining Magazine and Review* (London), I (January, 1872), p. 40.

21. Asbury Harpending, *The Great Diamond Hoax and Other Stirring Incidents in the Life of Asbury Harpending*, ed. by James H. Wilkins (San Francisco, 1913), p. 177.

22. Boston Mining Company, Nevada Gold District, Colorado Territory [prospectus] (Boston, 1863), p. 4; Prospectus of the Helmick Silver Mining Company of Colorado (Washington, 1870), p. 4; The Toiyabe Silver Mining Co. [prospectus] (New York, 1865), p. 30; Silver Bell Mining and Smelting Company, Ltd. [prospectus] (London, 1890); Prospectus of the Harmony Gold and Silver Mining Company of Nevada (New York, 1865), p. 14.

23. Apparently the original was in the prospectus of the Boston Mining Company, Nevada Gold District, Colorado Territory (Boston, 1863), p. 23. The Silver Mines of Nevada [prospectus] (New York, 1864), p. 12; The Economy Silver Mining Company [prospectus] (n. p., 1865), p. 4; Amador Consolidated Silver Mining Company [prospectus] (Boston, 1866), p. 25; Group of Valuable Silver Mines at Austin, Reese River, Lander County, State of Nevada [prospectus] (Boston, 1865), pp. 17–18; The Pah-Ranagat Central Silver Mining Co., Pah-Ranagat District Nye County, Nevada [prospectus] (New York, 1866), p. 12.

24. J. Ross Browne, *Adventures in the Apache Country: A Tour through Arizona and Sonora, with Notes on the Silver Regions of Nevada* (New York, 1871), p. 528; Henry B. Clifford, *Rocks in the Road to Fortune* (New York, 1908), pp. 210–11.

25. Quoted in *New York Express*, March 22, 1864.

26. Stephen Roberts to N. A. Garvin (December 5, 1878), copy, Roberts letterbook II, Bancroft Library, University of California, Berkeley.

27. *Mining World* (Las Vegas, N. M.), V (June 21, 1879); Eben Olcott to W. E. Newberry (September 6, 1895), copy, letterbook 23, Olcott MSS, New York Historical Society.

28. H. C. Sutman to Edward C. Watson (September 8, 1905), Goldfield (Nevada) Mining Companies MSS, I, Bancroft Library.

29. Unidentified clipping, October 29, 1863, Bancroft scrapbook LII, p. 23, Bancroft Library.

30. *Sixth Annual Report of the Secretary of Labor, 1918* (Washington, D.C., 1918), p. 13.

Suggestions for Further Reading

The following bibliography seeks to guide readers to our major sources, as well as suggest where to pursue further study of specific topics.

AKARD, MARGARET. *Margo with Her Ramblings from Arizona to Hawaii* (self-published in 1938). About half the book is devoted to the author's observations of pre-World War I Bisbee.

BAILEY, LYNN R. *Bisbee: Queen of the Copper Camps.* Tucson: Westernlore Press, 1983.

BENET, STEPHEN VINCENT. *The Beginning of Wisdom.* New York: Henry Holt and Company, 1921. Contains a chapter on the deportation in which Bisbee is thinly disguised as Frickett.

BOURKE, JOHN GREGORY. *On the Border With Crook.* New York: Scribner's, 1902.

BROWNE, J. ROSS. *Adventures in the Apache Country: A Tour through Arizona and Sonora, with Notes on the Silver Regions of Nevada.* New York: Harper, 1871.

BURGESS, OPIE RUNDLE. *Bisbee, Not So Long Ago.* San Antonio, Texas: Naylor Co., 1967.

BYRKIT, JAMES W. *Forging the Copper Collar: Arizona's Labor-Management War, 1901–1921.* Tucson: University of Arizona Press, 1982.

CANTY, J. MICHAEL, and MICHAEL N. GREELEY, eds. *History of Mining in Arizona.* Tucson: Mining Club of the Southwest Foundation, 1987.

CHISHOLM, JOE. *Brewery Gulch: Frontier Days of Old Arizona—Last Outpost of the Great Southwest.* San Antonio: Naylor Co., 1949.

CLIFFORD, HENRY B. *Rocks in the Road to Fortune.* New York: Gotham Press, 1908.

Cochise Quarterly. First issued in March 1971; it has carried many articles relating to Bisbee. It is published by the Cochise County Historical and Archaeological Society in Douglas, Arizona.

COLE, M. ELIZABETH. *Jottings from Overland Trip to Arizona and California* (privately published in 1908).

COX, ANNIE M. "History of Bisbee, 1877 to 1937" (M. A. Thesis, University of Arizona, 1938).

DAY, JAMES M., ed. *Morris B. Parker's Mules, Mines and Me in Mexico, 1895–1932.* Tucson: University of Arizona Press, 1979.

DEBO, ANGIE. *Geronimo: The Man, His Time, His Place.* Norman: University of Oklahoma Press, 1976.

DUBOFSKY, MELVYN. *We Shall Be All: A History of the Industrial Workers of the World.* New York: Quadrangle, 1969.

EPLER, WILLIAM, and GARY DILLARD. *Phelps Dodge, A Copper Centennial, 1881–1981.* Bisbee: Copper Queen Publishing Company, 1981.

FALK, ODIE B. *Tombstone: Myth and Reality.* New York: Oxford University Press, 1972.

FATHAUER, ISABEL SHATTUCK. *Lemuel C. Shattuck: "A Little Mining, A Little Banking, and a Little Beer."* Tucson: Westernlore Press, 1991.

FOSTER, JAMES C., ed. *American Labor in the Southwest: The First One Hundred Years.* Tucson: University of Arizona Press, 1982.

FRANCAVIGLIA, RICHARD V. "Copper Mining and Landscape Evolution: A Century of Change in the Warren Mining District, Arizona." *Journal of Arizona History* 23(1982): 267–98.

——— . *Hard Places: Reading the Landscape of America's Historic Mining Districts.* Iowa City: University of Iowa Press, 1991.

——— . *Mining Town Trolleys: A History of Arizona's Warren-Bisbee Railway.* Bisbee: Copper Queen Publishing Company, 1983.

HALL, LINDA B., and DON M. COERVER. *Revolution on the Border: The United States and Mexico, 1910–1920.* Albuquerque: University of New Mexico Press, 1988.

HOFSOMMER, DON L. *The Southern Pacific: 1901–1985.* College Station: Texas A&M University Press, 1986.

HOUSTON, ROBERT. *Bisbee '17: A Novel.* New York: Pantheon, 1979.

HULSE, J. F. *Texas Lawyer: The Life of William H. Burges.* El Paso, Texas: Mangan Books, 1982. Burges was a Phelps Dodge company lawyer during the deportation trial, and this book contains three chapters on the subject.

JORALEMON, IRA B. *Romantic Copper: Its Lure and Lore.* New York City: D. Appleton-Century Company, 1935.

KING, JOSEPH E. *A Mine to Make a Mine: Financing the Colorado Mining Industry, 1959–1902.* College Station: Texas A&M Press, 1977.

KLUGER, JAMES R. *The Clifton-Morenci Strike: Labor Difficulty in Arizona, 1915–1916.* Tucson: University of Arizona Press, 1970.

LANGTON, H. H. *James Douglas, A Memoir.* Toronto: University of Toronto Press, 1940.

LUCKINGHAM, BRADFORD. *The Urban Southwest: A Profile History of Albuquerque-El Paso-Phoenix-Tucson.* El Paso: Texas Western Press, 1982.

MARSHALL, JAMES. *Santa Fe: The Railroad that Built an Empire.* New York City: Random House, 1945.

MEINIG, D. W. *Southwest: Three Peoples in Geographical Change, 1600–1970.* New York: Oxford University Press, 1971.

MELLINGER, PHILIP. "The Beginnings of Modern Industrial Unionism in the Southwest: Labor Trouble Among Unskilled Copper Workers, 1903–1917." (Ph.D. Dissertation, University of Chicago, 1978).

MYRICK, DAVID F. *Railroads of Arizona.* Vols. 1–3. San Diego: Howell-North, 1975.

NAVIN, THOMAS R. *Copper Mining and Management.* Tucson: University of Arizona Press, 1978.

NEWTON, HARRY J. *The Pitfalls of Mining Finance.* Denver: Daily Mining Record, 1904.

NEWKIRK, WILLIAM W. "Historical Geography of Bisbee, Arizona." (M.A. Thesis, University of Arizona, 1966).

OFFICER, JAMES E. *Hispanic Arizona, 1536–1856.* Tucson: University of Arizona Press, 1987.

QUILLE, DAN DE [WILLIAM WRIGHT]. *The Big Bonanza.* New York: Thomas Y. Crowell Co., 1947 edition.

RANSOME, FREDERICK LESLIE. *The Geology and Ore Deposits of the Bisbee Quadrangle, Arizona.* Washington, D.C.: Government Printing Office, 1904.

RICE, GEORGE GRAHAM. *My Adventures with Your Money.* Boston: Gorham Press, 1913.

RICHTER, CONRAD. *Tacey Cromwell.* Albuquerque: University of New Mexico Press, 1974 reprint of 1942 edition. This novel brings turn-of-the-century Bisbee to life.

RIEGEL, ROBERT EDGAR. *The Story of the Western Railroads: 1852 Through the Reign of the Giants.* New York: Macmillan, 1926.

ROBERTSON, DONALD B. *Encyclopedia of Western Railroad History: The Desert States.* Caldwell, Idaho: The Caxton Printers, 1986.

SARGENT, CHARLES, ed. *Metro Arizona.* Scottsdale, Arizona: Biffington Books, 1988.

SMITH, DUANE A. "The Promoter, the Investor, and the Mining Engineer: A Case Study" *Huntington Library Quarterly* 39 (August 1976): 385–401.

——— . *Rocky Mountain Mining Camps: The Urban Frontier.* Lincoln: University of Nebraska Press, 1974 reprint of 1967 edition.

SONNICHSEN, C. L. *Colonel Greene and the Copper Skyrocket.* Tucson: University of Arizona Press, 1974.

SPENCE, CLARK C. *British Investments and the American Mining Frontier 1860–1901.* Ithaca: Cornell University Press, 1958.

——— . *Mining Engineers and the American West: The Lace-Boot Brigade, 1849–1933.* New Haven: Yale University Press, 1970.

SWAN, WALTER. *"me 'n Henry."* Marana, Arizona: Swan Enterprises,

1978. First-hand account of Bisbee and Cochise County in the early decades after Arizona statehood.

TAFT, PHILIP. "The Bisbee Deportation." *Labor History* 13 (Winter 1972): 3–40.

THRAPP, DAN L. *The Conquest of Apacheria.* Norman: University of Oklahoma Press, 1967.

VAUGHAN, TOM. "Borderland Chronicles," published weekly or bi-monthly in the Bisbee *Daily Review* since 1983.

WAGONER, JAY J. *Arizona Territory, 1863–1912: A Political History.* Tucson: University of Arizona Press, 1970.

WENTWORTH, FRANK L. *Bisbee With the Big B.* Iowa City: Mercer Printing Company, 1938.

YOUNG, OTIS E., JR. *Western Mining: An Informal Account of Precious-Metals Prospecting, Placering, Lode Mining, and Milling on the American Frontier from Spanish Times to 1893.* Norman: University of Oklahoma Press, 1970.

Photograph Sources

24 Bisbee Mining and Historical Museum: Accession No. 82.24.1.
Fly photograph.

27 Arizona Historical Society Library No. 61245.

28 Bisbee Mining and Historical Museum: Accession No. 080.138.22.
Fly photograph.

29 Arizona Historical Society Library No. 1226.

30 University of Arizona Special Collections.

32 University of Arizona Special Collections.

32 Bisbee Mining and Historical Museum: Accession No. 74.108.85.

34 Bisbee Mining and Historical Museum: Accession No. 081.141.30.

35 Bisbee Mining and Historical Museum: Accession No. 74.53.17.
Graves photograph.

36 Bisbee Mining and Historical Museum: Accession No. 79.97.92.
Fly photograph.

37 Bisbee Mining and Historical Museum: Accession No. 79.35.1.

39 Bisbee Mining and Historical Museum: Accession No. 74.53.7.

42 Bisbee Mining and Historical Museum: Accession No. 79.97.122.

44 Bisbee Mining and Historical Museum: Accession No. 80.44.1.
Buehman photograph.

45 Arizona Historical Society: Accession No. 15651. Fly photograph.

47 Bisbee Mining and Historical Museum: Accession No. 72.6.10.

49 Bisbee Mining and Historical Museum: Accession No. 72.15.5.

51 Bisbee Mining and Historical Museum: Accession No. 74.53.54.
Graves photograph.

52 Bisbee Mining and Historical Museum: Accession No. 74.53.38.

53 Bisbee Mining and Historical Museum: Accession No. 81.39.37.

55 Bisbee Mining and Historical Museum: Photo by Tom Vaughan.

56 Bisbee Mining and Historical Museum: Accession No. 80.38.43.

58 Bisbee Mining and Historical Museum: Accession No. 80.151.11.
Humphries photograph.

59 Bisbee Mining and Historical Museum: Accession No. 83.62.5.

60 Bisbee Mining and Historical Museum: Accession No. 74.107.78A.
GEHM photograph.

60 Bisbee Mining and Historical Museum: Accession No. 80.108.2.
Irwin photograph.

62 Bisbee Mining and Historical Museum: Accession No. 080.89.86.
Irwin photograph.

63 Bisbee Mining and Historical Museum: Accession No. 76.70.2A.

63 Bisbee Mining and Historical Museum: Accession No. 72.6.53V.
Fly photograph.

64 Bisbee Mining and Historical Museum: Accession No. 90.24.1. Sunbeam Studio photograph.

65 Bisbee Mining and Historical Museum: Accession No. 80.38.16. Irwin photograph.

66 Bisbee Mining and Historical Museum: Accession No. 80.115.21.

67 Bisbee Mining and Historical Museum: Accession No. 72.97.18. Humphries photograph.

68 Bisbee Mining and Historical Museum: Accession No. 74.107.25.

69 Bisbee Mining and Historical Museum: Accession No. 80.43.64. Nemeck photograph.

69 Bisbee Mining and Historical Museum: Accession No. 084.33.1.

70 Cochise County Historical and Archeaological Society, Douglas.

71 Bisbee Mining and Historical Museum: Accession No. 80.49.60.

71 Bisbee Mining and Historical Museum: Accession No. 74.107.76b. GEHM photograph.

72 Bisbee Mining and Historical Museum: Accession No. 72.6.53y. Fly photograph.

73 Bisbee Mining and Historical Museum: Accession No. 79.17.12. Humphries photograph.

73 Bisbee Mining and Historical Museum: Accession No. 75.11.35.

74 Bisbee Mining and Historical Museum: Accession No. 72.6.19. Markey photograph.

75 Bisbee Mining and Historical Museum: Accession No. 72.16.41.

76 Bisbee Mining and Historical Museum: Accession No. 83.18.17.

77 Bisbee Mining and Historical Museum: Accession No. 74.109.10.

77 Bisbee Mining and Historical Museum: Accession No. 80.150.6.

78 Bisbee Mining and Historical Museum: Accession No. 79.97.106. Miller photograph.

79 Bisbee Mining and Historical Museum: Accession No. 80.69.23.

80 Bisbee Mining and Historical Museum: Accession No. 79.104.7.

81 Bisbee Mining and Historical Museum: Accession No. 87.54.3. Irwin photograph.

82 Bisbee Mining and Historical Museum: Accession No. 81.98.107.

83 Bisbee Mining and Historical Museum: Accession No. 73.47.5; Crockett Collection.

84 Bisbee Mining and Historical Museum: Accession No. 80.138.1. Markey photograph.

87 Bisbee Mining and Historical Museum: Accession No. 80.43.150. Irwin photograph.

87 Bisbee Mining and Historical Museum: Accession No. 82.74; Riggins Collection. Fly photograph.

88 Bisbee Mining and Historical Museum: Accession No. 74.107.87.
Haynes photograph.

88 Bisbee Mining and Historical Museum: Accession No. 79.97.46.
Haynes photograph.

90 Arizona Historical Society. Feldman photograph.

91 Bisbee Mining and Historical Museum: Accession No. 79.97.80.
Fly photograph.

94 Bisbee Mining and Historical Museum: Accession No. 80.108.1.
Irwin photograph.

96 Bisbee Mining and Historical Museum: Accession No. 74.116.5.

97 Bisbee Mining and Historical Museum: Accession No. 80.38.19.
Humphries photograph.

100 Bisbee Mining and Historical Museum: Accession No. 74.53.36.

103 Bisbee Mining and Historical Museum: Accession No. 74.108.12b.

105 Bisbee Mining and Historical Museum: Accession No. 77.25.82.
Fly photograph.

106 Bisbee Mining and Historical Museum: Accession No. 79.97.48.

108 Bisbee Mining and Historical Museum: Accession No. 81.98.99.
Humphries photograph.

109 Bisbee Mining and Historical Museum: Accession No. 72.115.50.

111 Bisbee Mining and Historical Museum: Accession No. 79.97.78.
Fly photograph.

112 Bisbee Mining and Historical Museum: Accession No. 79.97.98.
Fly photograph.

113 Bisbee Mining and Historical Museum: Accession No. 80.151.3.
Humphries photograph.

114 Bisbee Mining and Historical Museum: Accession No. 85.70.2n;
Jeffrey Collection. Dowe photograph.

117 Bisbee Mining and Historical Museum: Accession No. 080.73.1.
Markey photograph.

118 Bisbee Mining and Historical Museum: Accession No. 83.28.7.

119 Bisbee Mining and Historical Museum: Accession No. 73.12.11j.

120 Bisbee Mining and Historical Museum: Accession No. 76.91.29n.

122 Bisbee Mining and Historical Museum: Accession No. 72.6.13.
Nemeck photograph.

123 Bisbee Mining and Historical Museum: Accession No. 72.59.102h.

124 Bisbee Mining and Historical Museum: Accession No. 74.107.41.
Fly photograph.

125 Bisbee Mining and Historical Museum: Accession No. 80.150.1.

126 Bisbee Mining and Historical Museum: Accession No. 75.41.5a.
Dix photograph.

126 Bisbee Mining and Historical Museum: Accession No. 76.91.28n. Dix photograph.

127 Bisbee Mining and Historical Museum: Accession No. 74.40.10. Dix photograph.

129 Bisbee Mining and Historical Museum: Accession No. 81.39.101.

Index

About the Contributors

CARLOS A. SCHWANTES is professor of history at the University of Idaho and author of several books and articles about the American West. He is currently writing a history of business and labor in the twentieth-century West.

TOM VAUGHAN is a native of Michigan who moved to Bisbee in 1977. His ongoing research into local history forms the basis for his newspaper column "Borderland Chronicles" as well as for other publications and public lectures. Vaughan is curator of Archival Collections at the Bisbee Mining and Historical Museum.

CHARLES S. SARGENT is associate professor of geography at Arizona State University. He has specialized in the study of urbanization in Latin America and the American West. He edited *Metro Arizona* (1988), a geographical history.

RICHARD GRAEME worked underground in the Bisbee mines for twelve years after graduating from Bisbee High School. He later completed a degree in geological engineering from the University of Arizona and was for a time Vice President of Operations of Sharon Steel's mineral division. He is now director of the Mining Remedial Recovery Company in Tucson.

DON L. HOFSOMMER is director of public history at St. Cloud State University in Minnesota. He has written extensively on the topic of railroads and railroading in the trans-Chicago West. Two of his recent books dealt with the history of the Southern Pacific Company and the Great Northern Railway.

CLARK C. SPENCE retired in 1990 from a long and distinguished career as professor of history at the University of Illinois. Through his many books and articles on hard-rock mining in the West, Spence has done much to define the field.